from the
bomb
to the
beatles

from the bomb to the beatles

Juliet Gardiner

foreword by
Terence Conran

COLLINS & BROWN

First published in Great Britain in 1999
by Collins & Brown Limited
London House
Great Eastern Wharf
Parkgate Road
London SW11 4NQ

3 5 7 9 8 6 4 2

British Library Cataloguing-in-Publication Data: A catalogue record for this book is available from the British Library.

ISBN 1-85585-664-6 (hardback edition)

Editor: Ginny Surtees and Mandy Greenfield
Original Design Concept: CD Partnership
Designer: Alison Lee
Picture Research: Philippa Lewis

Reproduction by Hong Kong Graphic and Printing, Hong Kong
Printed and bound in Portugal by Portuguesa

The images on the cover are from the BBC Archive, Corbis, Hulton Getty, Philippe Garner and Topham Picturepoint

contents

foreword

Above
**THE AWESOME TASK
OF POST-WAR
RECONSTRUCTION**
The devastation in
Coventry city centre
which was gutted by a
ten-hour long raid in
November 1940. 554
people were killed and
865 were seriously
wounded; a third of the
city's houses were
rendered uninhabitable; a
hundred acres of the
centre were razed,
including the Cathedral.
'Coventry is finished'
people said. But it wasn't.

The twenty years following the war were, for me, spent as a teenager progressing to adulthood. I think my generation was almost certainly the first to assert its independence so young. Britain came out of the war with a new Labour government, and it's clear that the British as a whole sensed and wanted change. Nonetheless, the impetus for that change came primarily from young people who passionately believed that the world could and should be a different place.

The spirit of optimism has to be set, of course, against the rather bleak realities of Britain in 1945: war-torn, bombed, grey, economically depressed, with little hope of an end to rationing. It doesn't seem too fanciful to suggest that over the next twenty years, Britain would – like photography – change from black-and-white to colour.

The Festival of Britain in 1951 was intended as a showcase for all that was dynamic and modern about the country, its Skylon a beacon that lit the way to a braver, brighter future. Like many young designers, I was inspired by the bravura and vision of Herbert Morrison and Hugh Casson, the Festival's director, and I worked on three or four exhibition stands, working day and night on a diet of black coffee and sausage rolls to keep me awake. Architecture and design magazines from America and Europe were filled with work by such people as Charles and Ray Earnes, Raymond Loewy, Alvar Aalto and Arne Jacobsen and it seemed that Britain, too, could be only moments away from embracing modernism.

How wrong I was – or, perhaps, how wrong we got it. For every inspired example of local authority housing, such as Pimlico and the Golden Lane estate in the City of London, there were dozens of soulless high-rises. And while hospitals, schools, factories and office buildings took advantage of new materials and methods of construction, the average

British household remained resolutely faithful to Edwardian notions of domesticity.

As Britain moved out of a period of absolute austerity, this failure to adopt new styles for the home came as something of a rude shock to me. Buoyed by the success of the Festival of Britain, I had set up my own furniture-making business. We had our first workshop in the basement of a house in Notting Hill. The room above ours was used as a rehearsal space by a ballet company, and every day we would make our furniture to the sound of feet thumping on the floorboards above. In the evenings, I would make deliveries of small pieces of furniture strapped to the back of my Vespa. It was all rather amateur, and very hand-to-mouth.

At around this time, I made my first trips to France and Italy. My eyes were literally opened to a different way of doing things – a less pretentious way of life, in which pleasure was often derived from simple things done well. Good earthenware pots, solid saucepans, salads dressed in olive oil and a squeeze of lemon juice, huge plates of pasta hungrily devoured by the extended *famiglia*.

These trips had and have continued to have a huge influence on me. Most immediately, they provided me with the inspiration to open a restaurant called the Soup Kitchen, just off Trafalgar Square, with a friend called Ivan Storey. The place was simply designed, with large blown-up steel engravings of pots and pans on the wall and it sold just four kinds of soup, french bread and cheddar cheese, apple flan made by a lady in Golders Green, and coffee – the last from the second machine in London. This was in 1953, when young people, especially, were beginning for the very first time to express their wants rather than just their basic needs.

Espresso coffee was to the fifties what marijuana was to the sixties, the drug of choice for a generation. It was all part

Right and below. 'MODERN WOMAN' Sketches in the magazine *Modern Woman* in 1947 showing a hint of a softening of fashion's silhouette, which had been taken to dramatic extremes by the French courtier Dior that year in his full, long, feminine 'new look'.

of a particular scene. Although I wasn't particularly active in the CND movement, I was sympathetic to it, as were a lot of designers and people involved in the arts. We were politically aware, keen to forge a brighter future, but not averse to having a good time.

One of my friends was something of a dandy: Brinsley Black first managed our furniture showroom in Piccadilly Arcade and then used to help out in the restaurant I'd opened on the King's Road, called The Orrery (my mother had to show him how to use a mop). Under Brinsley's sartorial supervision, we would go to Colliers, 'the fifty shilling tailors', where we would get ourselves some rather sharp suits made. I also possessed an overcoat with a velvet collar and red lining to the pockets, which I thought to be immensely chic. We even both appeared in the pages of *Tailor & Cutter*!

Nonetheless, when I neeeded to see my bank manager, I would dress up specially in a sober suit and I even bought a bowler hat for the purpose. Looking back, the fifties and early sixties seem like a period of great contrasts: Elizabeth David writing when food was still rationed; the establishment pomp of the Queen's coronation against the West End pazazz of Guys n' Dolls; CND and the Suez – which so outraged me that I got everyone I worked with to sign a letter to our local MP – versus the fairly debauched evenings drinking at Muriel's or in nightclubs such as the Piranha, the Sunset Room and the Saddleroom; Cold War politics side-by-side with James Bond espionage.

Equally you might argue that there were stark differences depending on your age and in which part of the country you lived. Whilst the media (and especially television) apparently brought us together, the old divides of the country, north and

Facing page
'THREE PEOPLE AT A TABLE' (1955)
Painting by John Bratby of fellow Royal College of Art student Jean Cook (whom he later married) and Brian Innes (right), former leader of the 'Temperance Seven' a jazz group that ironized '20s and '30s swing. Bratby saw his '50s work as 'dedicated to portraying an ugly, stark reality'.

Above left and right
INCORPORATING MODERNITY
Preview of the 1956 National Radio and TV Show at Earl's Court with 'Miss England, 1955' on the left and 'the original Yakity-Yak girl' on the right. A 1950's advertisement for laminated surfaces that makes life seem like a musical.

south, showed few signs of change. Retailers who visited my showrooms in the fifties, or Habitat when it opened in 1964, were usually sceptical about there being a domestic market for our furniture; and even those who admired what we were trying to do would dismiss it by saying that it was all very well for a select few people in 'swinging' Chelsea, but it would never work in places like Manchester or Leeds or Glasgow. With hindsight, the extent and pace of change between 1945 and 1965 seems huge, but at the time the forward momentum felt painfully slow.

The twenty years to 1965 saw immense social changes, and some of these directly influenced my determination to start Habitat: young people were leaving home before getting married; they had a greater disposable income than ever before; and there seemed to be a general will to make Britain more modern. I was certain that there were sufficient people who wanted to move away from the class-bound snobberies of provincial England and that they would embrace a new style of living if only they could afford it. In the early to mid-sixties that was still quite a small group of people: the media attention that the likes of Habitat and Biba enjoyed was out of all proportion to our number of customers. But it helped set a different agenda.

Although I hate labels such as 'the Swinging Sixties' and 'Cool Britannia', I suppose they help us to identify trends. If that's so, I think there's a pervasive argument that the King's Road/Beatles/Mary Quant/Habitat 'mini-quake' of thirty years ago planted the seeds for the cultural boom we have seen over the last two or three years. It will be interesting to see what the social historians in 2030 make of 'From the Beatles to Blair'!

Terence Conran

Facing page top left
'FROFFY COFFEE'
The Kaleidoscope Coffee Bar in Gerrard Street, Soho in 1963 in a part of the West End now known as Chinatown.

Facing page bottom left
'WE'RE ALL GOING ON A SUMMER HOLIDAY'
Vehicle for Cliff Richard's singin' and dancin' in a film about four London Transport mechanics who 'borrow' a double-decker bus for a continental *Summer Holiday*.

Facing page right
THE AVENGING FETISH
A leather-clad Diana Rigg practising her judo and karate techniques for the role of Mrs Peel, that she took over from Honor Blackman in 1965, in *The Avengers*, a long-running television series also starring Patrick MacNee.

Background
THE LIVERPOOL SOUND
Fans wave farewell to the Beatles in February 1965 as they fly off to film with Eleanor Bron. The film came to be called *Help!*

Left
YOUTHQUAKE
1960s fashion – geometric haircut, hoop earrings, black-and-white 'op art' PVC coat and bag snapped at the Rag Time Ball held at Wembley in November 1965.

the land of beginning again

DIG FOR ...

PLENT

GROW FOOD IN YOUR GARDEN OR ALLOTMENT

SELECTED SNOEK
DE SARDINAS EN A

Selected Snoek

Craven 'A'
FOR YOUR THROAT'S SAKE

'we found it actually was V Day from the porter'

**Above
VICTORY PARADE
(MAY 1945)**
Crowds swarm round the boarded-up statue of Eros in Piccadilly Circus. There was singing and fireworks, drinking and dancing in the streets to celebrate the end of the war in Europe, but the joy was tempered by the knowledge that the war had taken the lives of millions, and the youth of countless more.

**Facing page
'RUS IN URBE' (1946)**
Painting by Eliot Hodgkin. Dandelions and nettles rampage through the bombed churchyard of St Swithin's church in the city of London with the symbol of wartime survival, St Paul's Cathedral, in the background.

On 8 May 1945, Naomi Mitchison – who was one of the hundreds of men and women keeping a wartime diary recording the mood of the Home Front for Mass-Observation, the organization that had been taking the pulse of the ordinary people of Britain since 1937 – travelled to London from her home in Scotland. As the train steamed south, children climbed aboard wearing red, white and blue ribbons, and the sight of flags and bunting bedecking windows and fences as London approached made her suspect that the Second World War – at least in Europe – was officially over. But it was not until the train reached Euston that 'we found it actually was V Day from the porter'. [1] The announcement had been delayed by confusion and negotiation among the Allies (Britain, the US and Russia), and although word had leaked out the day before, King George VI was frustrated at going to bed on 7 May 'having

made my broadcast speech for record purposes with cinema, photography, and with no broadcast at 9 p.m. today!!' [2]

After lunch on 8 May the former diplomat and eternal socialite, Harold Nicolson, who was Conservative Member of Parliament for West Leicester at the time, strolled from his club in Pall Mall to the House of Commons to hear the wartime Prime Minister, Winston Churchill, announce the peace broadcast over loudspeakers to the waiting crowds.

'The whole of Trafalgar Square and Whitehall was packed with people. Somebody had made a corner in rosettes, flags, streamers, paper whisks, and above all paper hats. The latter were horrible, being comic. I also regret to say that I observed three guardsmen in full uniform, wearing such hats... And through this cheerful though not exuberant crowd, I pushed my way to the House of Commons... As Big Ben struck three, there was an extraordinary hush over the assembled

multitude, and then came Winston [Churchill]'s voice. He was short and effective, merely announcing that unconditional surrender had been signed and naming the signatories… "The evildoers," he intoned, "now lay prostrate before us!" The crowd gasped at this phrase. "Advance Britannia!" he shouted at the end, and there followed the Last Post and God Save the King, which we all sang very loudly indeed. And then cheer upon cheer.' [3]

Naomi Mitchison was in the crowds in the West End that Victory afternoon, but what she noticed was the exhaustion: 'Almost everyone was tired and wanting to look rather than do. They were sitting when possible, lots of them on the steps of St Martin's. Most people were wearing bright coloured clothes, lots of them red and white and blue in some form… Most women had lipstick and a kind of put-on smile, but all but the very young looked very tired when they stopped actually smiling.' [4]

The exhaustion and uncertainty mixed with relief and jubilation were hardly surprising. It had been a desperately long war. The price had been devastating: fifty-five million dead. Britain counted 30,000 lost on the battlefields and at sea and 60,000 killed on the Home Front. Half a million houses had been destroyed, and a further 250,000 were severely damaged; schools, hospitals and the social services were severely disrupted. Millions of people were in uniform or employed in war industries. Britain's debt – mainly to the US – was £3.5 billion, the largest in history, and two-thirds of the country's export trade had been lost. In effect, the economy was in a shambles and the task of rebuilding the country seemed almost insurmountable.

In his *Poems of an Ordinary Seaman* David Kendall, returning from the war in the Mediterranean, reflected on the task ahead:

After these years of war we cannot think
easily of the inevitable days…
we lack the courage to begin again

to make our new land, vision out our dreams
our fingers bleeding, building up the walls;
unhampered by the old world's decadent form
the shining towers rise into the sky…

Our minds are full
of war: let us erase the slate.

We have a right to live, enjoy our age,
sink back, for once, upon the cushions, make
our own particular castles, leave the rest
work for the future – we have had enough. [5]

Of course VE Day had only signalled the cessation of hostilities in Europe. In the Far East the terrible carnage went on for a further three months. But finally the journalist James Hodson was able to record VJ Day when, after the atomic bombing of Hiroshima and Nagasaki, Japan surrendered on 14 August 1945: 'The war is over.' Hodson went to talk to POWs (prisoners of war) who were undergoing rehabilitation at Hatfield House, the home of the Marquis of Salisbury, and were 'being helped to make the journey back to Civvy Street'. He identified with their fears: 'For months, or more often years (and sometimes five years), we have been isolated from normal life. This Britain to which we have come back has changed greatly. We're unsure of our former skills as professional men or craftsmen; sometimes uncertain too of ourselves in company, or with womenfolk, for we haven't been near them for so long. This new world we are plunged back into is a bit of a jungle. We're worried about our health, for we've not had enough to eat; we're worried whether we shall get a job…each of us has his own troubles, maybe concerned with wife or children, or the need for a house.' [6]

But although these problems were particularly acute for former POWs – especially those who had been in the Far East – this 'new world' was a challenge for all returning soldiers, and for those who had seen out the six years of wartime danger, hardship and privation at home, too. There was a longing to get back to normal – though no consensus about what 'normal' was any more – coupled with a conviction that the post-war world had to be a better and a fairer place. The hankering for a return to the supposed certainties of the pre-war world, which had been so evident – and so cruelly dashed – after the First World War, was absent.

'Will it be so again?' the poet Cecil Day Lewis asked. 'A poppy wreath for the slain/And a cut-throat world for the living? that stale imposture/Played on us once again?' [7]

The slate had to be wiped clean in 1945 and the manifesto on which the Labour Party fought the general election in July was 'Let Us Face the Future'.

Churchill had been anxious to continue the wartime coalition until Japan had been defeated, and the leader of the Labour Party, Clement Attlee, was disposed the same way. However, at the Labour Party Conference held in Blackpool on 20 May, 1945, it was clear that, as far as the grass roots were concerned, political consensus was over. Peace had brought a return to party politics and a wish to call to account the 'guilty men' of the 1930s, who were charged not only with nefarious diplomacy and a wilful failure to rearm in the face of the German threat, but with a callous indifference to social and economic problems, particularly as they affected the working man. As the journalist Anthony Howard has written: 'the dole queue was more evocative than El Alamein'.[8]

The Conservative campaign slogan 'Let him finish the job' found little accord in the country; the politicians of appeasement and unemployment were not to be the masters

Left
VJ DAY HEADLINE
The end of the war in Japan and the Far East. 'We met on VJ night,' wrote the poet John Heath-Stubbs, 'supposedly celebrating victory. The cloud over Hiroshima cast turbid reflections in the beer. We have lived in that shadow ever since.'

Below
'WE SHALL FIGHT IN THE CONSTITUENCIES'
The 'old warrior' faces the peace. Winston Churchill electioneering with his wife, Clementine, in his own seat of Woodford, Essex, on 26 May 1945 during the general election campaign.

of the post-war world and the Conservative Prime Minister, 'Winnie', with his boiler suit and stirring rhetoric, may have been an inspiring wartime leader, but was not seen as the man to build the future. As Tom Harrisson of Mass-Observation recognized: 'Millions…thought of Churchill, specifically, as a mighty support in dire necessity, a sort of intellectual deep-shelter, intended for emergency protection only.' [9]

The election was held on 5 July 1945: the results were delayed while the votes of nearly three million servicemen and -women came in. The outcome, announced on 26 July, was a resounding – and surprising – victory for the Labour Party. It was a landslide. The people had made their choice. Captain Richard Pim, who had run the map room in Churchill's bomb-proof wartime bunker beneath Whitehall, where the Prime Minister worked, 'turned quite grey' when he heard the news. But then he rallied. 'They are perfectly

entitled to vote as they please. This is democracy. This is what we have been fighting for.' [10]

Labour had won 227 seats and now held 393, to the Tories' 213, while the Liberals were reduced to just twelve; there were two Communist Party candidates returned and twenty-two Independent members. The Conservative vote had in fact held up reasonably well in their traditional strongholds in the shires and home counties: it was the Services' vote that went decisively against Churchill (as 'Bomber' Harris had warned him it would), as well as the men and women from the munitions factories and the ordnance depots, who had turned against pre-war politicians and policies. Churchill was dignified in defeat: 'I have laid down the charge that was placed upon me in darker times' – though a friend noted the ex-Prime Minister's musings that evening: 'It will be strange not to be consulted…upon the great affairs of State. I shall return to my artistic pursuits. Mary, get the picture I did the other day in France.' [11]

Attlee's wife, Vi, drove him to Buckingham Palace in their Standard 10: it passed through the gates fifteen minutes after Churchill's chauffeur-driven Rolls-Royce had swept out. The modernity of the occasion was underlined by the King, who responded to Attlee's announcement 'I've won the election' with: 'I know. I heard it on the six o'clock News.' [12] To the people Attlee promised, 'We are facing a new era. Labour can deliver the goods', as he flew off to the Potsdam Conference in Churchill's stead to confer with Truman and Stalin on the future shape of Europe.

When Parliament met on 1 August, Conservative members greeted their fallen hero with as rousing a rendering of 'For He's a Jolly Good Fellow' as their depleted ranks could muster. Labour MPs responded by singing 'The Red Flag' – although those members who could get through all the verses were few. It looked as if William Beveridge, in his report on social insurance, published in 1942 – which was to be the blueprint for the new government – had been right to insist: 'a revolutionary moment in the world's history is a time for revolutions, not for patching'. [13]

The Attlee government, with a Cabinet of experienced men (and one woman, Ellen Wilkinson – 'Red Ellen' of the Jarrow hunger marches), most of whom were over sixty, was committed to social and economic revolution. It was one that would abolish poverty. In the words of the hugely popular Beveridge Report (which had become a 600,000-plus bestseller after its publication in 1942), it was an attack on the five giants, inscribed in bold capitals, of 'WANT, DISEASE, IGNORANCE, SQUALOR and IDLENESS' on the road to national recovery. The plan was for a comprehensive welfare system, which Churchill described as

caring for the citizen 'from the cradle to the grave', with compulsory National Insurance contributions providing for child allowances and safeguards against the hazards of injury at work, disability, sickness, unemployment, old age and even death (in the form of widows' pensions).

Both main parties had endorsed the report, but it was obvious from the election results that the populace regarded Labour as the party most likely to implement it. The experience of wartime solidarity – when the burdens of bombs and rationing had been shared more or less equally, and when the imperatives of a wartime command economy for resources and services had given the State a greater regulatory and therefore interventionist role – had made such a comprehensive plan not only feasible, but expected. Indeed, the electorate's priorities, revealed by Gallup polls from 1942 onwards, had been housing (41 per cent); full employment (15 per cent); and social security (7 per cent); trailed by the nationalization of industry (6 per cent). [14]

But before any of the 'giants' outlined by Beveridge (by now an ex-MP himself, having lost his seat as a Liberal in Berwick in the election) could be slain, there was the immediate and massive problem of demobilization and the conversion of war industries to peacetime production. In 1945 some five million men and women were in the armed forces. At the end of the First World War demobilization had been determined by occupation, and this had led to civil unrest and mutinies, since it had effectively resulted in a 'last in, first out' strategy. A wiser course was adopted in 1945 of prioritizing by age and length of service. There were still criticisms of the pace at which men and women were returning to civilian life, which seemed unaccountably slow: the first 44,500 service personnel were home by the end of June 1945 and by the end of December one and a half

million had been demobilized, but it was not until January 1947 that this human aspect of dismantling the war effort was complete. [15]

Soldiers might have sung 'When I get my civvy clothes on/Oh! How happy I shall be' [16] in their wartime barracks, but the transition was often painful. Up to six years of khaki- or serge-wearing regimented life had left men unfit for civilian life, in both emotional and material ways. As James Hodson pointed out, 'they have usually built up an idealized picture of the country and home they had, and harsher realities are found hard to grow accustomed to. After the first three or four weeks of festivities another "crisis" period can develop. One reason may be that, instead of being at once accepted as "cock of the walk", the husband may find that his wife had gained new authority by added war responsibilities – care of children, struggling with the blackout and bombing, and perhaps on top of that earning good wages in a factory. He may secretly or openly resent this. She, on the other hand, may be jealous of his life overseas, which, despite its hardships, strikes her as rather "glamorous". Much tolerance and understanding are needed on both sides, so that in "resettling" the soldier, it is important to resettle his wife and family too.' [17] And, Hodson might have added, half a million of the demobilized service personnel were women, who had to make their own adjustments to a safer, but smaller and drabber, world.

All clothing was still rationed, with only 48 coupons a year (a 'débutante summer spot dress in rayon that looks like linen in blue, green, pink and stone' from Marshall and Snelgrove in Oxford Street took seven coupons, while a 'well-tailored coat in good materials including tweed' from the same store took eighteen). This meant that to accumulate sufficient points to acquire a civilian wardrobe (estimated at

Facing page
'WELCOME HOME' SOLDIER
But it wasn't an easy transition from war to peace – though there was plenty of advice. The BBC explained: 'We've got to scrap the idea that any of us is "coming back" to something we left.'

Above
CIVVY CLOTHES
The poet, Christopher Hassall, wrote that men chose their demob suits and diverged 'into the oblivion of freedom'.

223 coupons for a man and 213 for a woman) it would take a very long time before they were fully clothed. So each ex-servicewoman was given a starter pack of fifty-six clothing coupons and a money grant (and was told that she could keep her underwear),[18] while men reported to the Quartermaster's Store, where they were issued with a cardboard box containing a pinstripe or tweed demob suit of not very good-quality material, a raincoat, a shirt with two collars, a pair of cufflinks, two studs, a tie (various patterns), a hat, two pairs of socks and a pair of shoes. 'We don our old differences, hat by hat,' wrote the poet Christopher Hassall[19] as he watched the poignant return to civilian life of men made equal by the camaraderie of war.

Then there was the problem of a job; the ex-servicemen and -women were given a lump sum, depending on rank and length of service, were allowed eight weeks of resettlement leave and then directed to government offices, where they would be advised on future employment: there were vocational training schemes, some financial assistance to those who wanted to resume or embark on higher education – though nothing on the scale of the GI Bill, which gave US veterans the right to a college education – and grants and training for those who wanted to set up their own businesses. By law every employer was required to give back to a demobilized serviceman the job he had before the war. But firms had been bombed or turned over to war production; men who had not been called up had been promoted; men who had done menial work before the war had risen to positions of authority during the hostilities and found it loathsome to resume their humble former roles; women had come in to do the jobs that fighting men had left – and of course after six years away, many did not want to go back to old jobs and old ways. Compounding the problem was the

transition of war industries taking on another eight and a half million employees into peacetime production, which needed (at least at first) little more than half that number. The country was awash with drifts of people seeking jobs and homes. Demobilization could mean demoralization.[20] One woman who had joined the ATS from rural domestic service recalls, 'When we left the services we expected at first a lot was going to be different, a lot was going to be better. Of course it wasn't possible when you stop to think about it…but I think a lot of us were disappointed in the Britain that we came back to…nobody could make it change overnight into the Britain we wanted.' [21]

Of all the post-war shortages, the most desperate was housing. Lord Woolton, the wartime Minister of Food, whose name is forever associated with the famous wartime pie that bore his name, foresaw the problem at the height of

the Blitz: 'We are telling them now that they are heroes for the way in which they are standing up to the strain of the mighty bombardment – and it's true. I think they will keep on being heroes, but when the war is over they will demand the rewards of heroism: they will expect to get them very soon and no power on earth will be able to rebuild the homes at the speed that will be necessary.' [22] It was not only the Blitz and then the V1 and V2 bombs that had created the housing shortage: many pre-war dwellings had been condemned as slums, and a rebuilding programme was already under way at the outbreak of war. This came to an almost total halt, since priority was given to war production, with men and material being diverted to that. It was extremely difficult to obtain a building licence during the war, and neglected houses simply deteriorated further. The sharp rise in the birth rate during and immediately after the war only added to the pressure. A

government White Paper published in March 1945 suggested that some four million houses would need to be built in the next ten years.

All parties made housing an election issue in 1945, with Ernest Bevin pledging 'Five million homes in quick time' – a rash commitment, which the new Minister of Health and Housing, Aneurin Bevan, was committed to make good when Labour took office. Bevan's priority was subsidized local authority housing for rent – 'council houses' – but as building materials were in short supply, this meant tight controls being exercised on the private sector. Bevan permitted one private house to be built for every four local authority ones, and by the time the Labour government left office in 1951 only 18 per cent of houses built since the war had been for private sale.[23] In a further effort to conserve scarce materials, all repairs to private homes costing over £10 had to be licensed by the local authority. The bureaucracy, shortages of material and the slow demobilization of skilled labour meant that the programme was forestalled and, more than a year after the end of the war, many local authorities had not managed to build a single house. Local authority housing offices throughout Britain were besieged by queues of homeless people, by those living in slums that were not fit for human habitation, or by those who had been crammed in with family or friends for far too long. Seven to eight years was the average time that a London family might remain on the hated housing waiting-list, gradually building up the necessary points to be allocated a home of their own – and often having another baby, if that would help their ratings. Bevan's intention was to build high-standard council housing: he raised the minimum space allocation, prescribed upstairs toilets and insisted on houses being built on a human scale, with blocks of flats rising to no more than six storeys.

The Blitz had cruelly reduced the population of many inner-city boroughs, and town planners had resolved that this would be a wartime legacy on which they would build. Devastated and congested inner-city slum areas were to be redeveloped at a much lower density than in pre-war days, and the overflow population was to be drawn off into a rash of satellite new towns – Hemel Hempstead, Crawley, Stevenage, Harlow, Basildon – situated beyond the green belt encircling London, and others such as Corby, Peterlee, East Kilbride and Cwmbran: all built on the 'neighbourhood' model pioneered by the 'garden city' movement at the turn of the century, with open spaces, generous, tree-lined avenues and some thought given to how a collection of dwellings becomes a community. But again shortages of material and labour, the worsening economic climate and the overriding demands of the export drive meant that by the end of the 1940s most designated new-town sites were still fields of mud and piles of rubble.

In 1947 the first post-war Ideal Home Exhibition was held at London's Olympia. Its star attraction was the 'Village of Beginning Again', which featured a display of six prefabricated houses, one of which was made of aluminium produced by an aircraft firm for the Ministry of Supply.[24] These prefabs had become part of the post-war topography: 'temporary' matchbox dwellings cheaply erected, they were practical and basic, but had good-quality fittings and a small cottage garden. By the end of 1948 nearly 150,000 of these 'rabbit hutches' had been erected, and in some cases this stop-gap accommodation served as a family home for thirty years. In 1944 the *Daily Mail* had commissioned an extensive survey of the 'house that women want'.[25] Four and a half million women responded that they did not necessarily want to get out of the kitchen, but they certainly did want to make it a more pleasant place in which to work, with bigger windows and – that dream of women facing a future without domestic servants, or simply exhausted from the hard work and necessary inventiveness of wartime housework and cooking, combined with a family and job – 'labour-saving equipment', a fitted kitchen, a built-in bath (upstairs) with fittings that 'did not need polishing'; and 90 per cent wanted a house or bungalow and a private garden. But for several years this remained a dream for most women. It was not until 1949 that the Ideal Home Exhibition was actually able to mount a display of ideal homes, and the 'Pavilion of Beautiful Things' replaced the 'Village of Beginning Again'. Even then a reviewer of the exhibition sympathized: 'Of the thousands who throng to the exhibition, many are still eagerly looking for a home, not so much an ideal home, but any sort of home in a world that is starving for houses.'[26]

Facing page
UTILITY FURNITURE
Furniture production was the most rigorously supervised aspect of the government's Utility scheme because it used a precious wartime and reconstruction commodity – timber. The designer Gordon Russell was put in charge of a scheme to mass produce furniture; controls were not lifted until 1948 and the scheme ended in 1952.

Above
ROYAL WEDDING (1947)
On 20 November 1947, Princess Elizabeth, heir to the throne, married her cousin, Prince Philip of Greece, in Westminster Abbey. It was a right royal occasion with one of the largest gatherings in the twentieth century of regnant and exiled monarchs.

marguerite patten

Marguerite Patten taught the nation to cook in the post-war years.

'At the end of the war, women were exhausted and dispirited by the constant battle to get ingredients they needed to cook for their families. No one expected rationing to go on for so long. It lasted longer in Britain than in Germany. The biggest problem was meat. All people wanted was a good British roast – and that's just what they couldn't have.

There was the problem of cooking and shopping. Lots of young women had never been taught to cook – they had gone straight from school into the services. And they had to learn how to shop too – and housewives had to relearn. There was just no choice in the '40s. It wasn't a question of what did you want to cook. It was more what could you get to cook.

But there was a tremendous interest in cooking. So many service men and women had served overseas and they came back with new culinary ideas – it's always been said that the 8th Army discovered scampi in Italy – and of course Dublin Bay prawns were as good as anything fished out of the Adriatic'.

How to make your best-ever short crust pastry

PASTRY is easy to make if you handle the dough *carefully* to keep it cool, use the correct proportions of fat, etc., and bake at the right temperature.

Ingredients: 8 oz. flour—preferably plain, although self-raising makes very good pastry, 4 oz. fat—preferably 2 oz. margarine and 2 oz. cooking fat, OR all margarine or all butter, pinch salt, water to mix.

N.B. If using lard or cooking fat use only 3½ oz.—more gives a crumbly pastry that is difficult to handle.

1. Sieve flour and salt together. Cut fat into small pieces and put into flour.

2. Rub with the tips of the fingers only, until the mixture looks like fine breadcrumbs. Do not over-handle.

3. Gradually add enough cold water to bind—the correct amount is 2 tablespoons to 8 oz. flour. Too much water gives a sticky pastry, which will be tough when baked, less, a very crumbly pastry, which is difficult to handle and roll out.

4. Dust the pastry board and rolling-pin lightly with flour, roll out pastry and use as in individual recipes.

Remember: . . . When a recipe says "4 oz. short crust pastry" it means pastry made with 4 oz. flour, etc.

. . . When a recipe says "Bake the pastry case 'blind'" it means bake it while empty.

It was not only houses of which the British were starved. For six years it had been possible to respond to the demands for goods and services with the reprimand 'Don't you know there's a war on?' In the first years of peace, however, the enemy was harder to identify and calls to pull together and make do and mend were wearing thin. James Hodson reported at the end of August 1945: 'the conditions of war in some respects continue. You need only make a long railway journey in England to become aware of it. I travelled last Sunday to Newcastle-on-Tyne. The journey which in peacetime took four hours now took eight and a quarter. No food on the train. No cups of tea to be got at the stops because the queues for this remarkable beverage masquerading as tea were impossibly long...no taxi to be got [at the station]. My hotel towel is about the size of a pocket handkerchief, the soap tablet is worn to the thinness of paper, my bedsheets are torn.'[27]

Another journalist, Susan Cooper, wondered, 'After the war and the victory, where was the transformation scene?'[28] 'We still bathed in water that wouldn't come over your knees unless you flattened them; we still wore clothes with the ugly "Utility" half-moons on the label. Chewing carrots for sweets, we still said avidly to our parents: "Tell us about pre-war days", and wondered at stories of chocolate cigars and pineapple that didn't come out of tins... It was...the hope of release from the long grinding privations of wartime life...release from the small, dull makeshift meals, from darkness and drabness and making do, from the depressing, nerve-aching, never-ending need to be careful. For a great many people, war had meant the same kind of food, clothes, living conditions as the thirties: now, the vitality of Labour would whisk them out of both. The housewife knew that she would have to be patient a little longer, whipping up her mock cream from cornflour and margarine; but there was a good time coming soon. Well fairly soon.' [29]

But it wasn't: 'austerity' – the word that was still hovering on the lips of the President of the Board of Trade, Sir Stafford Cripps, when he became Chancellor of the Exchequer in November 1947 – was to persist right into the 1950s. Recovery did not mean a flow of goods to the individual consumer; it meant backs to the wall (once more) to 'get Britain going again', with a 'massive export drive', particularly after President Truman had summarily cut Lend Lease, the US aid that had essentially enabled Britain to win the war, in the immediate aftermath of VJ Day. The economist J.M. Keynes was despatched to Washington to beg or borrow for Britain's economic survival. The terms of the loan he managed to negotiate meant that a fiscal squeeze had to be clamped on domestic consumption, in order that production would be channelled for export – and, given the dollar-rich US hegemony of world markets, this was to be a long and uphill struggle.

By 1948 rations had fallen well below the wartime average. The usual allowance per week for a man was just thirteen ounces of meat, one and a half ounces of cheese, six ounces of butter and margarine, one ounce of cooking fat, eight ounces of sugar, two pints of milk and a single egg. [30]

In February 1946, dried egg, which had been a leathery wartime cooking staple of countless cakes, puddings and filling batters, disappeared from the shops. Such was the paucity of alternatives that an immediate campaign was mounted for its return. This gave momentum to a women's protest movement, the League of Housewives, which had been started in June 1945 by Mrs Iris Lovelock, a vicar's wife from South London. She had been apoplectic on behalf of her fellow-sufferers and had persuaded her husband to permit

SPAM 'N' PANCAKES

ANY MORNING is a good morning for pancakes—and piping hot fried SPAM. Here's how: easiest is to add liquid to your favorite prepared pancake mix; or, sift together 3 tsp. baking powder, ½ tsp. salt, 1 tsp. sugar and 2 cups sifted flour. Combine 2 well beaten eggs with 1½ cups milk. Then add flour mixture and beat until smooth; add 2 tbsp. melted shortening. Spoon on hot griddle and bake until first bubbles break, then turn. Makes 2 dozen small cakes.

Facing page
MANAGING THE COUPON BUDGET
Ensuring that the family was well fed was a complicated legacy of wartime austerity that lasted into the 1950s. Mrs Whitham, mother of sixteen children, puzzles it out in June 1945.

Left
ADVERT FOR SPAM
This ubiquitous wartime sustenance persisted into the meat-rationed peace with enterprising suggestions of how to serve it.

Below
SUPPLEMENTING THE RATIONS
Housewives queue for horsemeat outside a Brixton shop in January 1947. Eaten on the Continent, horsemeat was not usually considered human fare in Britain, but times were hard.

GROW FOOD IN YOUR GARDEN OR GET AN ALLOTMENT

the church hall to be used for the first of many protest meetings. The government duly conceded. But as dried eggs were reconstituted, bread was put on ration, although, as Churchill was quick to point out, even during the darkest days of the war, bread – that essential filler for hungry people – had been freely available. The new weekly ration was the equivalent of two large loaves per adult and one per child, with additional allowances for some twelve million people, mainly manual workers. And if all the additional form-filling and coupon-clipping were not bad enough, the loaves were increasingly unpalatable, grey-coloured and tasting of chalk, and there were mutterings that the main ingredient was not flour at all, but cattle feed. [31]

Fruit was scarce – and expensive – and the only people who could be sure of getting soft fruit and any variety in their vegetables were those who had continued to 'dig for victory'

in gardens, smallholdings, allotments and railway embankments – anywhere that a row of peas or beans and a few canes of raspberries could be encouraged to grow. Shops were largely empty of goods, with queues snaking from every store when supplies were expected; women were still darning worn lisle stockings, or continuing the wartime trick of smearing gravy-browning (or even wet sand) on their legs to look like nylons, which were in even shorter supply now that the GIs had left; beer was weak, whisky unobtainable; and even the advertisements were beginning to sound a little desperate: 'Won't it be nice when we have lovely lingerie, and Lux to look after our pretty things?'; 'Please continue to show forbearance with your suppliers…Better times will come when there will be more White Horse [whisky] and we shall all be glad'; 'All Heinz 57 varieties will be coming back – one by one'.

Facing page
BANANAS AGAIN
The first post-war consignment of bananas arrived in Britain in 1946. A current popular song enquired 'When Can I Have a Banana Again?' and the arrival of the cargo seemed an early – and misleading – symbol of a return to normal.

Above
'DIG FOR VICTORY' AND AFTER
Government propaganda encouraged continuing self-sufficiency by growing vegetables in gardens, backyards or allotments to supplement post-war food shortages.

'It was an Annus Horrendus'

'It was an Annus Horrendus,' said Hugh Dalton, the Chancellor of the Exchequer, of 1947. The winter of 1946–7 was the worst of the whole century. Snow fell in December and by the end of January the entire country was paralysed by ice and snow. Twelve-hour blizzards raged, and thousands were snowed in by drifts for days. Transport came to a standstill while snow-ploughs battled to keep pathways open. Power cuts were frequent: it was forbidden to switch on electric fires between 9 a.m. and midday and between 2 and 4 p.m.; the Third Programme (now Radio Three) was suspended, as were television transmissions – and greyhound racing. Years of clothing rationing meant that coats were worn and thin against the bitter cold and shoes let in the rain and snow. The freeze continued until the middle of March, with Scotland completely cut off by the worst storm in living memory, ten-foot snow drifts blanketing England and Wales, with thousands of acres of corn destroyed by frost, and sheep and cattle dead in the fields.

Manufacturing industry had ground to a virtual halt; industrial unrest in the mines had meant that coal production was still half a million tons short, and it was often impossible to get transport the supplies that there were: by the end of February 1947, 1.75 million men were officially out of work, with a further half a million 'stood off from employment' but still being paid[32]; several power stations had been forced to close for lack of coal and the ground was frozen so solid that parsnips had to be dug up with pneumatic drills. Then, just as it seemed that the freeze was over, in mid-March heavy rain mingling with melting snow on iron-hard ground caused severe flooding, which washed away the crops over thousands of acres in the fens, flooded parts of the London Underground (and cut off water supplies

to the capital) and caused further devastation and loss of life throughout the country. It seemed that things could hardly get worse: the government advised, 'Smoke your cigarettes down to the butt' and added 'it may even be good for your health', but put up the tax on tobacco anyway; newspapers shrunk to four pages with the ban on timber imports; and a similar restriction on petrol meant that the basic petrol allowance was abolished. Clothes coupons were reduced, and it became a criminal offence to have an electric fire on in the summer – not that that was any hardship, since the coldest winter in memory was followed by the hottest summer, with polio scares keeping children away from municipal swimming pools, and hardly any domestic refrigerators to keep food cool.

In April that year, the writer and critic Cyril Connolly compared Britain to the US: 'Here…most of us are not men or women but members of a vast, seedy, overworked, over-legislated, neuter class, with our drab clothes, our ration books and murder stories, our envious, strict, old-world apathies and resentment – a care-worn people. And the symbol of this mood is London, now the largest, saddest and dirtiest of the great cities, with its miles of unpainted half-inhabited houses, its chopless chop-houses, its beerless beer pubs…its crowds mooning around the stained green wicker of the cafeterias in their shabby raincoats, under a sky permanently dull and lowering like a metal dish-cover.'[33]

The Labour government used all its ingenuity to combat the shortages and the shortfall in post-war expectations: first it introduced whalemeat as a meat substitute: it looked like beef steak but tasted like oily fish, and most housewives soon decided that even Spam was better than that. Then it introduced snoek, a 'long, slender fish weighing up to

Above left
FREEDOM OF THE ROAD
Petrol rationing meant there was every incentive to get on your bike and enjoy the delights of the peacetime countryside.

Above
HEATWAVE
After the bitter winter of 1947, the spring brought floods and the summer a heatwave. The *Meteorological Magazine* reported that 'At Oxford the mean temperature for the month was the highest for August since records were first taken in 1815', and the British public headed for the beaches.

Snoek

In October 1947, 10 million tons of snoek were imported to replace Portuguese sardines and tinned salmon with this South African fish which saved foreign currency. Though the Minister of Food confessed that he 'had never met a snoek', research revealed that it was a large, fierce tropical fish like a barracuda, with a row of fearsome teeth. It was said to taste like mackerel, but the British housewife was not impressed. Thousands upon thousands of tins piled up, unsold despite the fact that they were cheap and used few coupons.

eighteen pounds'. Snoek came in tins – ten million of them imported from South Africa – and the government published tempting recipes to persuade the population that the addition of some spring onions, syrup and vinegar would create a delicious 'Snoek piquante'. But the housewife remained sceptical and, even when snoek came off points in 1949, it did not sell; and in 1951 'a mysterious quantity of tinned fish came onto the market labelled "selected fish for cats and kittens",[34] selling at tenpence a tin.

If the government was ingenious, so were the people. An exhibition staged in 1946 at the instigation of Sir Stafford Cripps (who was a keen weekend carpenter himself) and organized by the Council for Industrial Design, which had been set up in 1944 to encourage good design, was called optimistically 'Britain Can Make It' (moving on from the wartime slogan 'Britain Can Take It'). It was staged to demonstrate that swords could be turned into ploughshares and that British manufacturers were capable of producing 'goods as suitable for peacetime as were the weapons the country produced for war'.[35] The exhibition was held in the Victoria and Albert Museum, whose exhibits had still not returned from wartime storage – and which had no windows, a problem solved by Cripps, who diverted the entire glass supply of the capital to rectify this. The exhibition was clearly a daunting task 'with no materials yet to make new things, and no skilled labour, with plenty of designers still in the forces, with an understandable dislike to show the old 1938 things again, and an equally understandable dislike to show new things not yet in production'.[36]

Yet it was a great success, with exhibits entitled 'From War to Peace', where the exhaust stub of a wrecked Spitfire was displayed alongside a new type of saucepan in front of a background of bomb-blasted London picked out by shafts of

light. It was the poet John Betjeman whose voice provided the commentary for models of 'the Working Class Utility Kitchen', 'the Middle Class Kitchen with Dining Recess', the 'Suburban Living Room for a hard-up curate' (whose wife clearly collected modern pottery).[37] The public loved it: one and a half million people formed yet another patient queue to ogle the future – and 60 per cent of those anxious to see the new designs were under forty. But the exhibition's success did not stop them giving 'Britain Can Make It' their own label, 'Britain Can't Have It'; nor, in similar vein, did it stop them joining the Housewives' League in an explosion of frustration about scarcity and what seemed more and more like 'control with no planning', with a life regulated by forms, coupons, points, permissions and licences.

There were, of course, those who prospered while others fumed. The 'spiv' was a phenomenon of the early post-war

Above
'BRITAIN CAN MAKE IT'
But Britain can't have dainty shoes, as displayed at the Exhibition in November 1946 to a group of goods-starved Scots on a trip to London. The Exhibition was a tribute to Britain's recovering post-war manufacturing – but most of the products had to go for export.

years: an alert opportunist, a showy racketeer who worked either side of the boundaries of the law to bring people what they could not get but badly wanted – at a price. Nylons, whisky, cigarettes, imported goods, foreign currency, perfume, little luxuries – the spiv (no one seemed quite sure where the name came from) flourished in a climate where there was in any case a feeling that to flout regulations was a way of showing that you were still fighting, not ground into subservient obedience by a growing army of civil servants and petty regulations. The law too often seemed an ass, with a greengrocer being prosecuted for selling a couple of extra pounds of potatoes that would have gone mouldy if they had not been cooked straight away, and a pig farmer brought to book for slaughtering one of his pigs a day before the date on the licence said he should.[38] 'Helping yourself' if you came across stuff that had 'fallen off the back of a lorry' now seemed to make good sense in looking after your own interests because no one else would. Property thefts rose from a value of two and a half million pounds in 1938 to thirteen million in 1947; in 1948 *The Times* reckoned that there were upwards of 20,000 deserters out there without a ration book, who were living all right anyway; and the number of indictable offences rose from just over a quarter of a million in 1937, to well over double that by 1947, and the Recorder of London despaired of 'this distemper of dishonesty which has swept over the country in the last few years until people have lost sight of the difference between right and wrong'.[39] But despite such portrayals as that of the young psychopathic spiv, Pinkie, played by Richard Attenborough in the screen version of Graham Greene's *Brighton Rock* which came out in 1947, to many in post-war Britain, the spiv could be enjoyed as the 'prince of the wide boys', good for nylons or chocolates for the wife, or a long-

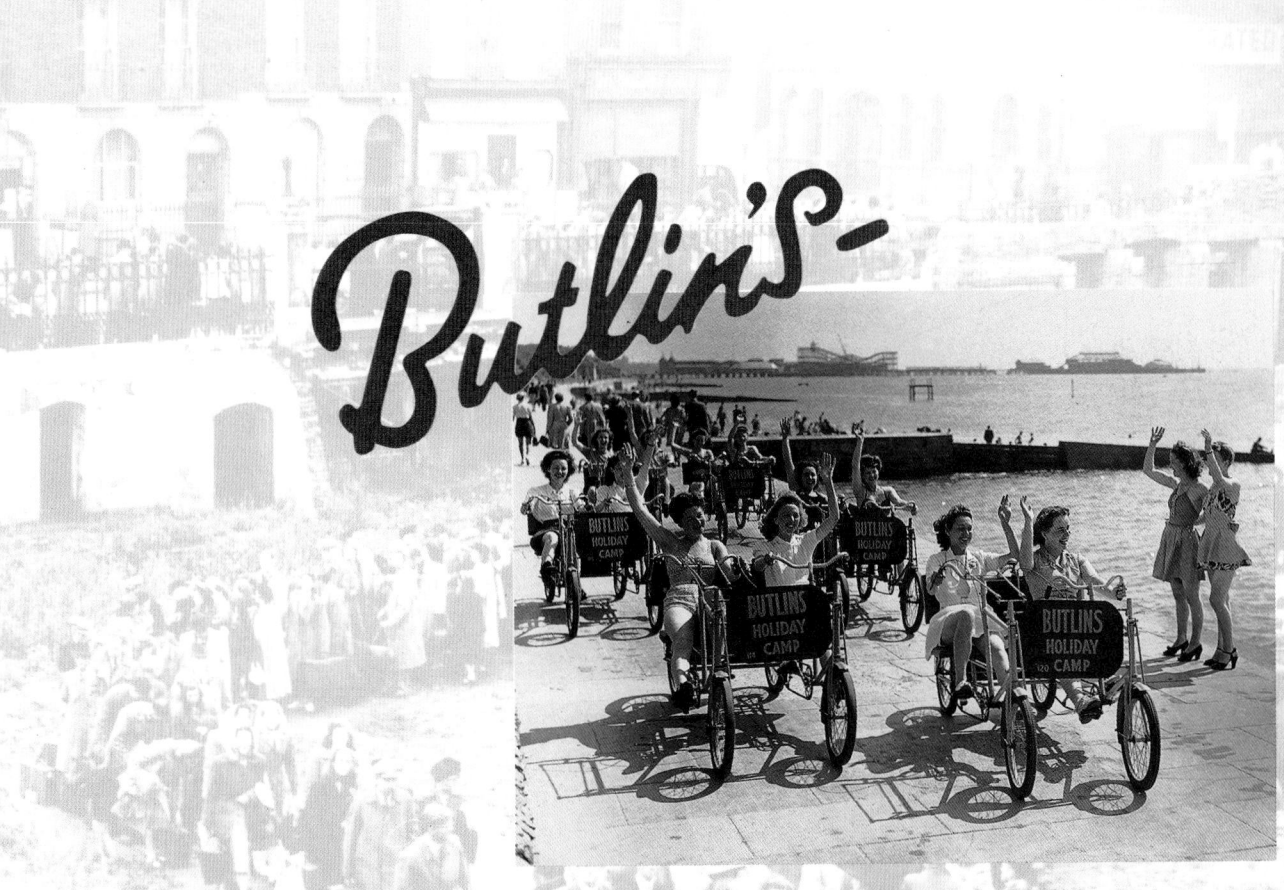

coveted bottle of whisky covertly offered in the pub. 'Flashily displaying all the suppressed energies of the back streets, [spivs] were an unconscious, dramatic form of civil disobedience that millions of English people found endearing.'[40]

A weekly column in the *People* chronicled the latest spivs' tricks, but not everyone was amused. Virginia Graham wrote:

Young man in a purple suit
balanced on pointed ginger feet
at the corner of Denman Street [in Soho],
selling illicit silk stockings
with fancy clockings
in the furtive half light
of a dirty drunken Piccadilly night;
young man in a purple suit
doing a little business on the side;
it was not for you my son died.[41]

If the unity and uniformity that had seemed so comforting in wartime had come to seem repressive and stultifying in peacetime, there were other, legal ways of expressing some individuality, of having some fun. If the only furniture that could be obtained – and that only under licence – was Utility furniture, it was at least of high quality and functional, and could always be 'customized' with the addition of carvings or trims to bring things back to the 'Jacobean', which has long seemed the British design default-position. As builders and decorators were employed in essential rebuilding, the late 1940s saw the start of the 'do-it-yourself' craze, which meant 'having a go' with paint and the new decorative finishes that were starting to be developed.

With tight currency controls and restrictions on foreign travel, holidays abroad were impossible for all but the wealthiest who 'knew somebody', but the 1938 Holidays

Facing page top
SPIVS
Selling nylons out of a suitcase in Oxford Street in 1950, a 'spiv' at work. These 'wide boys' operated a black market, which gave the public what they wanted – illegally.

Facing page bottom
THE BRYLCREEM BOY
The *Daily Telegraph's* cricket correspondent commented of cricketer Denis Compton that 'his happy demeanour and his good looks completed the beau ideal of a sportsman'.

Above
BUTLINS
Special trains ran every Saturday night taking holidaymakers for a week of activity-packed outdoor fun in one of the seaside camps.

with Pay Act meant that, by the end of the war, over 80 per cent of the labour force was covered by the provisions of the Act. An enterprising young man who liked to be known as 'Mr Happiness' had spotted the trend before the war, and in 1936 he opened his first holiday camp in Skegness, followed by one in Clacton a year later. So efficient was 'Billy' Butlin at building and equipping his complexes that he was commissioned to build more for government use.

At the end of the war he bought back from the government the camps he had built, and opened them as holiday, rather than army, camps offering a week of fresh air and regimented fun. For an all-in price holidaymakers got chalet accommodation, three meals a day (though of course visitors had to hand in their ration books to obtain these) and non-stop entertainment. Television was in its infancy: it was the heyday of the cinema, with one-third of Britain's population 'going to the pictures' at least once a week in 1946.[42] But Hedy Lamarr or Rita Hayworth was unlikely to be persuaded to do a season at Filey or Pwllheli, so Butlin's slogan was 'The Stars You Have Heard But Rarely Seen' and campers were entertained by such radio luminaries as Tommy Handley of ITMA fame, Tessie O'Shea, Richard Murdoch, Kenneth Horne and the Beverley Sisters, but also the San Carlo Opera imported to perform *La Bohème* (it was considered that soldiers who had fought in Italy had acquired a taste for opera there[43]) and the London Symphony Orchestra conducted by Vic Oliver. The classless camaraderie of war and the notion of everyone enjoying the same entertainment persisted in such enterprises.[44]

In February 1947 the magazine *Harper's Bazaar* proclaimed excitedly: 'Paris is more feminine than ever. Paris rounds every line' above a report on the Dior fashion show that introduced what came to be called 'the new look'. This consisted of 'a tight, slender bodice narrowing into a tiny wasp waist, below which the skirt burst into fullness like a flower. Every line is rounded…shoulders are gently curved. Bosoms are rounded out with padding…Every house in Paris shows day skirts twelve inches from the ground, with even longer skirts for the afternoon.'[44] It was a far cry from Utility clothes with their practical skirts, and from military styling, which used the minimum of material. *Vogue* saw it as a metaphor: 'We in England will not partake of [the new look] very fast at present [but]…let us in small things as well as great hold to the idea of one world civilization, from which we cannot be cut off by anything but the closing of our own minds.'

Sir Stafford Cripps did not find the idea heady at all; instead he tried to persuade the British fashion industry that it would be helping the economy if it kept the short skirt popular in Britain, and women trade unionists and MPs – including the redoubtable Bessie Braddock – weighed in with words like 'ridiculous', 'wasteful', 'frivolous'. It was like a revival of the rational dress movement of the 1890s, with suggestions that long skirts 'caged' women and would encumber active, equal, professional lives. But it was a hopeless Canute moment. By the spring of 1948 Fenwicks was advertising a 'ballerina suit, with softly rounded shoulders, page-boy nipped-in jacket, gaily swinging skirt to give the new fashion look. Exciting colours and gay mixtures. 18 coupons, £5. 12s. 6d.', while Richard Shops were offering similar temptations for 'pocket Venuses…our Ballerina skirted coat with a Victorian bodice that accentuates your waist and your feminine curves. Soft velour in lovely pastel shades. 15 coupons, £6. 2s. 7d.'

Soon rather a lot of items were being described as 'new-look', from family cars, which were beginning to roll off the

Facing page
THRILLING ESCAPISM
The melodrama *The Wicked Lady* starring Margaret Lockwood and James Mason was one of the top British box office grossers in 1946.

Left
ESCAPE FROM AUSTERITY
The archetypal elegant model, Barbara Goalen, in a 1950s British version by Susan Small of Dior's 1947 'new look', with nipped-in waist and long, full skirt.

Below
US IMPORT
Jiving to the beat of Humphrey Lyttleton's band playing New Orleans Jazz in his basement club at 100 Oxford Street, in November 1949.

Above
AN END TO DRABNESS
Advertisements for cigarettes and sheer nylon stockings in the early 1950s presage a supposedly more leisured and glamorous lifestyle for women than the workaday lisle hosiery of the war and years of austerity.

Facing page
SHOWCASING BRITAIN
The Lansbury Estate in Poplar, east London, an example of 'live architecture' which took a bomb-damaged area and rebuilt it as part of the Festival of Britain, to show what 'New Britain' would be like.

production line, to new-look housing, new-look furniture, new-look daffodil species – and even a new-look Labour Party, with younger men like Hugh Gaitskell (elected for South Shields in 1945) and Harold Wilson (the youngest Cabinet Minister when he joined the government as President of the Board of Trade in September 1947; Attlee was alleged to have regarded him as 'a possible high-flyer') coming to public attention. These new-look politicians edged out those who, in the face of daunting odds, had achieved great advances in social welfare, including family allowances, the doubling of pensions, comprehensive National Insurance and the introduction on 5 July 1948 of a National Health Service, plus a partially achieved shopping list of nationalization. But the war in Korea that broke out in June

1950 made even peace seem less secure, and the reforming zeal of the radical post-war years seemed to be trickling into a distrust of planning and direction, and a growing enthusiasm for the private sector, individual enterprise and the delights of a consumer society.

In October 1951 the Labour government was defeated in the second general election in less than two years – despite more people having voted Labour than ever before. The rejected wartime leader, Churchill, took the helm again. But in May that year the exhibition for which Labour's Home Secretary, Herbert Morrison, had lobbied and had described as 'a pat on the back for the British people' – the Festival of Britain – had opened on a bomb-site next to Waterloo Station.

Architecture at Poplar

hardy amies

Right
POST-WAR ELEGANCE
Hardy Amies *circa* 1950.
'I once said that our
motto could be: 'Less
than Art and more than
Trade'. I had this, perhaps
rather pompously,
translated into Latin as:
*Impare arte, negacio
superior*'.

Facing page left
AN AFTERNOON DRESS
Made in periwinkle blue
and with a hat by Simone
Miram, this 1948 Hardy
Amies' design was 'the
new long length' which
'permits much more
décolleté' – presumably
since it was only the
ankles visible below.

Facing page right
A NIGHT AT THE OPERA
An Amies-design formal
evening dress of 1948 in
'100% British material' of
stiff and burnished rayon
'which reflects olive green
and bronze lights', and
with a 'slight [velvet]
bustle at the back'.

The couturier Hardy Amies, a fluent linguist involved in military intelligence in the Second World War, was seconded from military duties for a time in 1940, at the request of the Board of Trade, to design for the overseas market in an effort to earn much-needed hard currency for the British war effort. He also designed 'Utility' garments for the domestic market.

In November 1945 he opened his first business in bombed-out premises in London's Savile Row, and established himself as one of the two top British post-war designers.

At first the collections were largely for export, and for this reason Amies was able to obtain fabrics that were hard to come by in the austerity years in order to produce the tailored, tweed clothes that became his signature: 'clothes that made an English woman look good in town and country'.

In 1950, the then Princess Elizabeth, paid a visit to Amies' salon to choose outfits for her tour of Canada, and as the Queen's dressmaker 'by appointment' Amies has designed clothes for numerous royal tours and public occasions – including 'a gown that stunned the nation' and which made the front page lead in the *Daily Express* in May 1965.

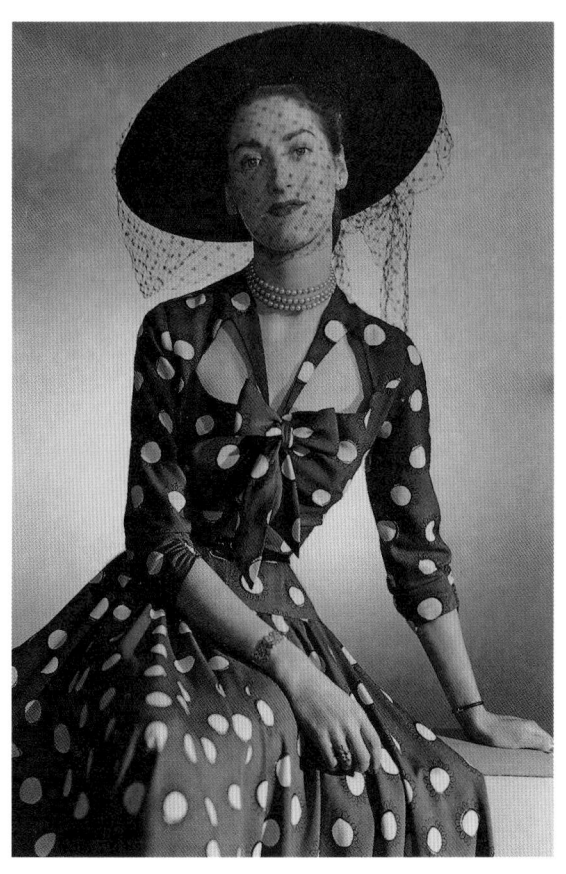

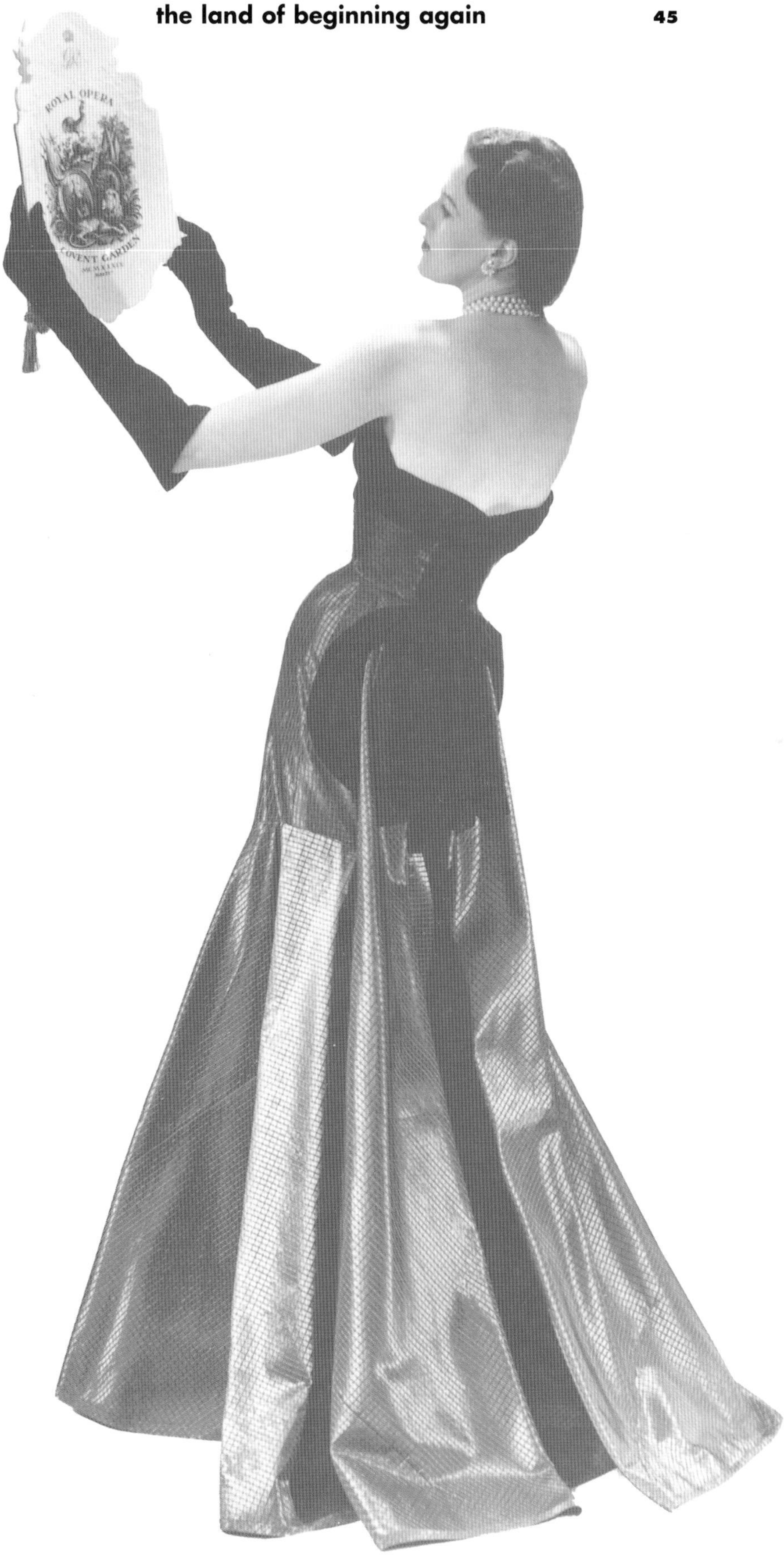
ROYAL OPERA
COVENT GARDEN

FESTIVAL OF BRITAIN 1951

ARIEL
The Modern Motorcycle
1958

Is there leisure in your life?

Like every other housewife, you would like to be able to relax from time to time. That is just what a Leisure-planned and Leisure-equipped kitchen would enable you to do, by reducing your work and saving your time.

LEISURE KITCHEN PLANNING SERVICE
You can obtain free and without obligation a plan and artist's impression of how your kitchen would look with Leisure. You would enjoy working with Leisure equipment, which, with its beautiful coloured Porcelain Enamel or Leisure 'Warwrite' and gleaming Stainless Steel, is so practical and such a delight to the eye.

ingham Road, Long Eaton, Nottingham
et W.1. Telephone: Regent 8355

LEISURE Kitchens

the atomic age

The
Hydrogen
Bomb

HER MAJESTY'S STATIONERY OFFICE
NINEPENCE NET

the promise of the atom

Peter Sellers · George C. Scott
in Stanley Kubrick's

Dr. Strangelove

Or:
How
I Learned
To
Stop
Worrying
And
Love
The
Bomb

the hot-line suspense comedy

also starring Sterling Hayden·Keenan Wynn·Slim Pickens and introducing Tracy Reed...
Screenplay by Stanley Kubrick, Peter George & Terry Southern Based on the book "Red Alert" by Peter George
Produced & Directed by Stanley Kubrick·A Columbia Pictures Release

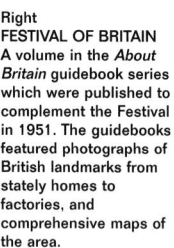

Right
FESTIVAL OF BRITAIN
A volume in the *About Britain* guidebook series which were published to complement the Festival in 1951. The guidebooks featured photographs of British landmarks from stately homes to factories, and comprehensive maps of the area.

Below
ANOTHER AGE, ANOTHER DOME
A drawing of the Dome of Discovery on the south bank of the Thames, part of the Festival of Britain exhibition.

Facing page
FESTIVAL TIME
A knitted Festival jumper showing the Festival logo featured on the cover of *Illustrated*, 1 May 1951 on the eve of the Exhibition opening.

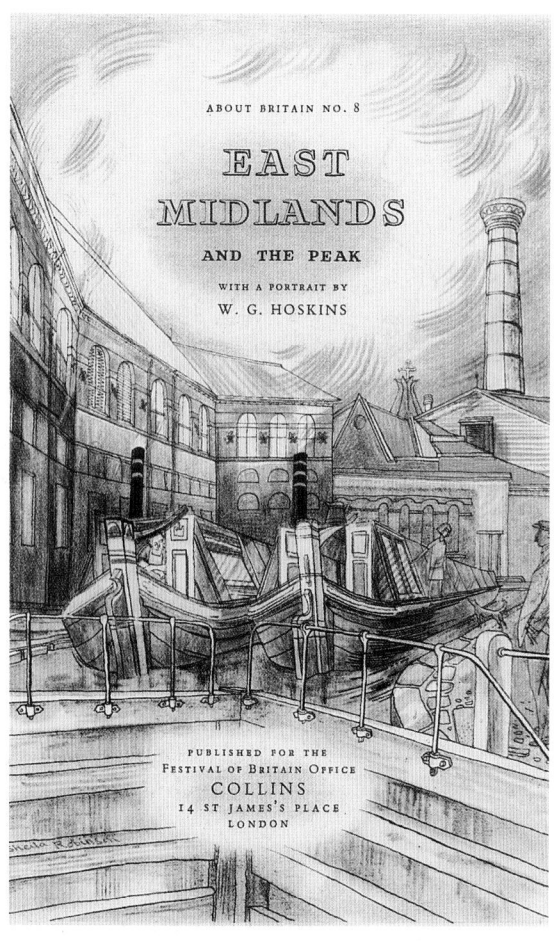

ABOUT BRITAIN NO. 8

EAST MIDLANDS

AND THE PEAK

WITH A PORTRAIT BY
W. G. HOSKINS

PUBLISHED FOR THE
FESTIVAL OF BRITAIN OFFICE
COLLINS
14 ST JAMES'S PLACE
LONDON

'The Festival [of Britain] is nation-wide. All through the summer, and all through the land, its spirit will be finding expression in a variety of British sights and a great range of British sounds. Taken together, these will add up to one united act of national reassessment and one corporate reaffirmation of faith in the nation's future,' explained one of the official guide books to the Festival,[1] and went on to explain just how it had all come about. 'It was in 1947 that His Majesty's Government decided that there should be displays to mark the centenary of the Great Exhibition of 1851, in the Arts, Architecture, Science, Technology and Industrial Design; so that this country and the world could pause to review British contributions to world civilization in the arts of peace.'[2]

The Festival might have been worthy in its intent, but it was nothing like as dull as the guide made it sound. Harold Nicolson went on the first day with his wife, Vita Sackville-West, and the couple were 'entranced from the first moment. It is rather a nuisance that we keep on running into the King and Queen, but nevertheless we enjoy it uproariously. It is the most intelligent exhibition I have ever visited. I have never seen people so cheered up or amused, in spite of a fine drizzle of rain.'[3]

The writer and playwright Michael Frayn saw its real importance: 'The Festival was a rainbow – a brilliant sign riding the tail of the storm and promising fairer weather. It marked the end of the hungry 'forties, and the beginning of an altogether easier decade.'[4]

The Great Exhibition Centenary Committee had begun its work in 1947: it was the responsibility of Herbert Morrison, Lord President of the Council (who, incidentally, was the grandfather of the inspiration of Britain's millennium festivities, Peter Mandelson), and its Director General was

WEEK ENDING MAY 5 1951   EVERY WEDNESDAY THREEPENCE

ILLUSTRATED

FESTIVAL TIME

'The Festival was a rainbow – a brilliant sign riding the tail of the storm and promising fairer weather'

Gerald Barry, who, as editor of the *News Chronicle*, had been lobbying for such an event almost since VJ Day. It would be 'a tonic to the nation', Barry urged, and no one could deny that this was needed. A number of interlocking committees were set up to bring this national 'bread and circuses' affair to fruition. Although, as it was 'a British affair, it had to be rather concentrated on the arts and the sciences…because Herbert Morrison was in it, he wanted the British people to have fun. He wanted it to be a fun thing, which made it unique…among all great exhibitions. He wanted the people to participate in it, he didn't want it to be a "them and us" affair. He wanted the teaching side of it, which was about science and so on, to be played down, and a great deal of jam spread over the pill.'[5]

There never was an overall blueprint and for a long time the site was uncertain: Olympia and Earls Court were already booked; a huge field at Isleworth was considered, but rejected on the grounds of cost; the director of the Victoria and Albert and the other South Kensington museums were reluctant to shut their museums again for two or three years, since it was not so long ago that they had reopened; a proposal for 'recoverable standard shedding' in Battersea Park was thankfully dropped – and finally in 1948 twenty-seven acres of marshy, derelict, willowherb-filled bomb-site, on the south bank of the Thames adjacent to Waterloo Station and dissected by the railway bridge to Charing Cross, was chosen.

Though Barry intended the Festival to be awash with 'fun, fantasy and colour', it was never intended to be what anyone might consider to be vulgar. As Michael Frayn diagnosed, 'It was scarcely the British of the working-classes that was being fêted. Apart from Herbert Morrison…there was almost no one of working-class background concerned in planning the Festival, and nothing about the result to suggest that the working-classes were anything more than the lovably human but essentially inert objects of benevolent administration. In fact Festival Britain was the Britain of the radical middle-classes – the do-gooders; the readers of the *News Chronicle*, the *Guardian* and the *Observer*; the signers of petitions; the backbone of the BBC. In short the Herbivores, or gentle ruminants, who look out from the lush pastures which are their natural station in life with eyes full of sorrow for less fortunate creatures, guiltily conscious of their advantages, though not usually ceasing to eat the grass.'[6]

Furthermore, the Director was astute: 'One mistake we should not make, we should not fall into the error of supposing we were going to produce anything conclusive. In this sceptical age, the glorious assurance of the mid-Victorians would find no echo.'[7] So, meeting 'on hilltops, in gardens, round a log-fire, wherever half a dozen people could foregather and talk…clambering among rubble and cement mixers, amid the uproar of cranes and pile drivers, in over-heated railway carriages and under-heated motor cars, tearing around the English landscape…in mayoral parlours, on fog-bound airfields, in lecture halls, youth centres, and standing on street corners waiting for a bus',[8] the planners planned. It was an impressive line-up of talent that heralded the renaissance of British architecture and design and confirmed the State's patronage of the arts. Some fifty architects and over a hundred designers were drafted away from the job of reconstruction, rehabilitation and Utility production to construct something new and modern and amazing for the delectation of Festival-goers.

The team of architects and designers, led by Hugh Casson and Misha Black, designed a series of pavilions to house exhibits that narrated the story of 'the land and the people of Britain'. They were linked by piazzas where visitors could get – if not a pizza – at least a cup of tea and a plate of chips and peas. Influenced by Le Corbusier in his earlier period, the young architects and designers had a manifesto for modernism – and a penchant for neo-brutalist concrete. There was an aesthetic for every detail, from the litter bins, signposts and cutlery to the ducks selected for the ornamental lake.[9]

The sculptor Michael Ayrton fashioned an exegesis of 'The Elements of the Source of Power'; painter Felix Topoloski executed a 'Cavalcade of Commonwealth' on a railway arch; Lynn Chadwick created a hanging mobile, Eduardo Paolozzi designed a fountain and Reg Butler a spiky wrought-iron birdcage; Jacob Epstein sculpted a gilded bronze 'Youth Advances' to stand outside the Homes and Gardens Pavilion; Victor Passmore tiled a swirling 'jazz' mural in ceramic, which 'exploded' on the side of the Regatta

Above
**FEATURING THE
FESTIVAL**
A souvenir Festival of
Britain edition of *The
Illustrated London News*
published on 12 May
1951, showing symbolic
figures of industry and the
arts linking the world to
the South Bank site far
below. painting by
Terence Cuneo.

Restaurant.[10] The door handles in this restaurant 'were bronze hands modelled by Mitzi Cunliffe, which [her fellow-sculptor] Barbara Hepworth refused to touch as she associated them with amputation'.[11] Henry Moore produced a bronze 'Reclining Figure' and Barbara Hepworth herself both an abstract sculpture and two monumental limestone figures called 'Contrapuntal Forms', which stood atop a podium outside the Dome of Discovery, a giant umbrella structure designed by Ralph Tubbs, which housed a microcosm of the whole world – including 'outer space'.

Then there was the skylon – a poet's name for 'a vertical feature, a symbol of triumph and gaiety piercing the sky'.[12] It was a giant aluminium exclamation mark, the prize-winning design of the young architects Moya and Powell, which seemed to hover in the sky without visible means of support – 'just like Britain,' the wits said.

'The South Bank contains a new sort of narrative about Britain: an Exhibition designed to tell a story mainly through the medium, not of words, but of tangible things.'[13] Upstream from Hungerford Bridge, the pavilions told 'the story of the Land of Britain and of the things that the British have derived from their land...downstream from Hungerford Bridge [the circuit of pavilions] relates the story of the People of Britain in the context of their more domestic life and leisure.'[14] However, the pavilions were 'placed in a certain deliberate sequence on the ground...and within each Pavilion, the displays are arranged in a certain order,' explained the guide book. But in keeping with the spirit of the new age, it allowed that 'this is a free country; and any visitors who, from habit or inclination, feel impelled to start with the last chapter of the narrative [expressed in the pavilions or the guide book] and then zigzag their way

backwards…will be as welcome as anyone else. But such visitors may find that some of the chapters will appear mystifying and inconsequent'.[15]

The upstream pavilions were bound to be somewhat museum-educational in character, with excursions around 'the rich and varied wild life that inhabits these islands' and demonstrations of 'how the British have drawn on their natural resources to produce raw materials for industry'.[16] But these pavilions gave the goods-starved visitors dreams to die for. There were to be 'no stunts, but real goods to go into real shops and so be available for real people', decreed the director of the Council for Industrial Design, which oversaw all the designs, as his colleagues scoured the country for well-designed furniture, fabrics, pottery, glass and domestic appliances. In total 10,000 objects were displayed representing the work of 3,500 firms.[17]

But it was not all didacticism. The intention was that the Festival should be a 'people's show' – and that meant fun for everyone. In addition to the pavilions there were bamboo vistas and arcades, elaborate tea pavilions, which owed a lot to the artist John Piper and the cartoonist Osbert Lancaster; there was an art competition for which prominent contemporary artists were provided with a large canvas and simply told to get on with it: Lucien Freud was a winner with his 'Interior near Paddington', but neither Michael Ayrton nor John Minton was placed, and Francis Bacon did not even enter; there was the 'Lion and Unicorn Pavilion' dedicated to the odd and the whimsical, for which the poet Laurie Lee was hired to write the captions. The Lion and the Unicorn, which were modelled in straw like corn dollies, bore the legend: 'we are…twin symbols of the Briton's character. As a Lion I give him solidity and strength. With the Unicorn

hugh casson

Above
HUGH CASSON
Hugh Casson with a plan
of the Festival site in
October 1950. 'The nation
was alerted to
possibilities and
opportunities hitherto
undreamed of. But the
real achievement of the
South Bank was that it
made people want things
to be better, and to
believe that they could be'.

Facing page
THE DOME OF
DISCOVERY
Designed by Ralph Tubbs,
a huge, 365-foot diameter
dome was the centrepiece
of the South Bank site,
and was a horizontal
contrast to the 300-foot
'vertical feature' of the
skylon – 'vivid, bright
and shining, hanging
miraculously in mid-air...
a symbol of hope,
triumph and gaiety
piercing the sky'.

'I was a latecomer to the team...collected to devise and run [the Festival of Britain]... One day we were summoned...to look at the South Bank site...on paper it looked marvellous – centrally placed, with good communications and within sight of Big Ben and Trafalgar Square. It was too good to be true, we said. It was...it was tiny...it was cut in half by...Charing Cross Bridge...most of the upstream site was dominated by a mountain of bomb rubble...nobody knew what or where services existed and there was only one tree... "Just the job", we said at once. "Never mind the complications, just look at the view".

"Is it as you expected?" asked the Queen [at the inauguration]. 'The only answer was "Yes" – but it wasn't. It was much, much better. It was serious and irreverent, gay, brightly-coloured and, if you agree with Bertrand Russell's description of intelligence as "the role of finding a means for realising an end by passion", it was an *intelligent* exhibition. For six months it was the most exciting place in London – 27 acres of battered buildings and mud flats miraculously transformed into a new world'.[18]

Above
FESTIVAL LOCOMOTION
The Far Tottering and
Oyster Creek Branch
Railway which transported
visitors around Battersea
Pleasure Gardens.
Designed by Rowland
Emett, the long-funnelled
engines which were
"dedicated utterly to never
giving one puff it two will
do", pulled carriages on a
15-inch track between
whimsical stations, and
all were a realisation of
the spidery drawings
that had been appearing
intermittently in *Punch*.

[which was engaged in a complicated device that let doves out of a 'colossal rattan birdcage'] he lets himself go.'[19]

Upstream from the exhibition in Battersea Park was a re-creation of the eighteenth-century pleasure gardens of Vauxhall, Cremorne and Ranelagh (its creation had involved cutting down a number of trees in the park 'late at night, having all the machinery there to cut the trees into logs and remove them by the morning' and disguising the stumps with pots of geraniums).[20] Young women dressed like Nell Gwyn offered oranges, cajoling 'come, gentle people, buy', and 'acrobats and aerial artists will give free performances at intervals throughout the day…the extensive floor of the Dance Pavilion [where people often danced in the rain and the autumn chill wearing overcoats and trilby hats] provides short sessions throughout the day…in the six-acre Amusement Park beside the Big Dipper and the Rotor, the ride that defies gravity…there is a Tree-top walk leading through the branches to a platform which gives a fine view of the gardens…there is a Clock Tower with working models which perform as each quarter strikes. There is a grotto in the form of four caves which represent the elements of Wind, Fire, Earth and Water. Rowland Emett has designed a complete railway in miniature 500 yards long [called the Far Tottering and Oyster Creek Railway], with all his characteristic fantasy…in the evenings the gardens will be transformed by the most spectacular and unusual displays and there will be nightly displays of fireworks.'[21]

There had been the usual calls for the postponement or cancellation of the Festival: the Beaverbrook papers, the *Daily Express* and the *Evening Standard*, began calling it 'Morrison's Folly' and inviting their readers to send in postcards saying why they thought the Festival should be called off (few did). An architect pronounced that the South

Bank site was too small and predicted that thousands would fall into the Thames in the crush. But, just like Prince Albert a hundred years earlier, the organizers ignored the jeremiads and the Festival was 95 per cent ready on time, despite the extremely unpropitious circumstances of its post-war construction. It had cost £8 million, which by any reckoning was pretty cut-price. King George VI opened it from the steps of St Paul's on 3 May 1951 (it had been suggested that the royal couple should perform the ceremony on Tower Hill and travel to the South Bank in the Royal Barge, but the King declined, saying that the Tower had far too many bloody associations for the royal line, and anyway the barge leaked). *The Times* reported 'People in Joyous Mood' and the next day, in pouring rain, the gates were opened to let in the first of what would be eight million visitors. The Festival closed at the end of September: Gracie Fields – who insisted on being paid in dollars – was the star attraction, but as the crowds belted out 'Auld Lang Syne' and then stood for the National Anthem as the Festival flag was lowered, their King, who had opened the Festival, was in the early stages of dying just a mile or so across the river.

The Labour Party, under whose rather remote auspices the Festival had been planned and held, was out of office the month after it closed, and there was an unseemly political rush to clear away the evidence of its success. 'I am unwilling,' declared the new Minister of Works, David Eccles, 'to become the caretaker of empty and deteriorating structures.'[22] The Festival Hall, a long-awaited London concert hall with its 'contemporary' interior of wood-clad walls, projecting boxes for the audience, decorative screens, superb acoustics and laminated plywood chairs, was the only permanent structure. Apart from that a café and a couple of other structures were the only constructions allowed to remain.

Above
THE ROYAL FESTIVAL HALL
The first public building to be built in Britain since the war, and the only permanent building on the South Bank Exhibition site, was a desperately-needed large space for music in London. The inaugural concert was on May 3 1951 and the Hall's acoustics were much admired: the audience did not hear trains thundering over the adjacent Hungerford Bridge.

Right
Right
LANSBURY ESTATE
A brave new post-war world. Plans are drawn up for the 124-acre Lansbury Estate in Poplar where 'people will live under conditions far happier, more spacious and convenient than in times gone by'.

Below
PLANNING FOR THE PEOPLE
A sketch of the Lansbury Estate showing one of the two schools 'which are the most modern in the country'. The Estate, which was an example of 'live architecture' at the Festival of Britain, was planned to be 'self-supporting, at least with regard to local needs...with a market-place and shopping centre, a Church, three schools (among them a nursery school), and a home for old people'.

The Marquis of Bath had been fairly interested in taking the skylon for Longleat, and there was the inevitable offer of a million dollars from the US if that and the Dome of Discovery were shipped across the Atlantic. In the end the site was saved for car parks and one of the least distinguished office blocks in the capital, before it began to fill with other artistic housings a couple of decades later, while the skylon was chopped up and turned into ashtrays.

But the Festival was more than the sum of the London sites: there was also a Land Travelling Exhibition, which toured the country 'with a fleet of lorries' and a 'Festival Ship', the *Campania*. It told 'the same story as the South Bank but in miniature' when it docked at coastal towns from May to October, and all over the country 'Festival events were arranged…in spontaneous expressions of citizenship', from ubiquitous displays of historical pageantry to basketball in Colchester and madrigals on the river at Cambridge; and the parish council of a Kent village dug up the turf of the Kentish Downs among the Nissen huts, bomb craters and a wartime airstrip into the shape of Abram Games' Festival logo – simplified a bit of course.[23]

Just as 'new' had become a hopeful catchword at the end of the 1940s, so 'Festival' came to encompass more than a collection of exhibition sites. It was, as one of the official guides said, 'the occasion for a national spring-cleaning, for repointing and repainting the Town Hall, gilding the church clock, for planting window boxes, flower baskets and temporary gardens, for painting the street lamps, decorating the streets and floodlit buildings.'[24] At the same time 'rural and urban district councils have planned more ambitious schemes…like a new sewerage system or changing the street lights from gas to electricity… Houses, cottages and clubs have been built for old-age pensioners. Playing fields and sports clubs have been made or improved… There are places where 1951 will see the foundation stone of the new Town Hall or where a new park will be opened for the first time… In some places, a village hall has been built and in others, where money has yet to be found, the events arranged by the local Festival may open the account.'[25] And, in a note to warm the hearts of the 'ruminants', the guide book proclaimed, 'this is an appropriate moment to offer a report on local progress in housing, schools or public health and there could be no better year for beginning new enterprises in various fields of local government. Many public buildings, roads, parks, recreation grounds will bear the figure "1951" as a witness of the inspiration which this Festival will have given to projects already in progress. Some corporations have planned to hold "Open House" for those interested in local government and others have arranged exhibitions showing the history of public administration in their community.'[26]

It was, as the guide said, 'an act of national autobiography, cities and towns throughout the country are presenting their own account of themselves'.[27] There were still shortages and privations: the incoming Conservative Party talked in aspirational terms about a 'property-owning democracy', since only some 200,000 houses had been built by 1947 and the majority of these had been by local authorities – though the 1949 Housing Act dropped the words 'for the working classes'.[28] And the demand for homes was growing. In 1948, 177,000 more marriages took place than houses were built, so until the late 1950s many young couples started off married life in their parents' (usually hers) back bedroom. Divorce, that present-day divider of homes, rose dramatically from 9,970 petitions in 1938 to its post-war peak of 47,041 in 1947 with, for the first time, more women than men seeking a divorce.

Left
FIRST RESIDENTS
The first family moved into the LCC showcase, Lansbury Estate, on 14 February 1951. Mr Albert Snoddy, his wife, two children and mother-in-law left their former Poplar home which was to be demolished as part of the slum clearance programme, and moved into a brand new flat with a (minimally) fitted kitchen.

The Lansbury Estate in Poplar was completed by the London County Council as a showcase for the Festival. It was praised as 'friendly architecture', and one of the first tenants to move in, a gas fitter with six children who had been on the waiting list for 'years before the war', thought his new home was 'about the best thing I've ever come across'.[29] But for thousands of others the wait for a home of their own dragged on into the late 1950s. And if you were lucky enough to get a house or flat, there was still the problem of furnishing it. After 1948 controls on furniture production and design were relaxed, and it became easier to buy items other than the plain Utility designs that were all that was available in the immediate post-war years, but it was not until the fall of the Labour government in 1951 that production of Utility furniture ceased. Newly-weds were given dockets that entitled them to an allocation of furniture, but this was rarely

Above
'WHEELS OF OUR OWN'
During the 1950s, private car ownership doubled. The blueprint for Harlow New Town just after the war, allowed one garage for every ten houses: by the time it was built the ratio was one car to every two houses.

Right
SCHOOL MILK
Children drinking their free school milk in September 1952. The scheme ensured that all primary school children, regardless of home circumstances, would gain from the nutritional benefit of milk.

sufficient for their needs and the choice was invariably severely limited. 'I hated green,' said a Lambeth woman, 'but green damask chairs were all that were available, so green it had to be.' Those who were eventually rehoused were often not much better off, since the new homes consisted of small rooms that would not accommodate a sturdy walnut dining table or a piano. And the new homes were arranged differently: gone were the parlour and dining room, to be combined into a living room with dining alcove, while the kitchen and scullery became a 'working' fitted kitchen.

Rationing did not finally end until 1954, fourteen years after its introduction and nine years after the end of the war. Bread rationing had ended in July 1948; in January 1950 milk rationing was suspended; in May that year hotels and restaurants were freed from the five-shilling meal maximum, and the restriction on the number of courses they could serve was lifted; clothes had come off rations in March 1949 in a 'bonfire of controls', in the words of Harold Wilson (whose wife, Mary, was photographed in the press tearing up her clothes ration book). That same month neon lights went up again over cinemas, theatres and restaurants in London. Sweets and chocolate no longer required coupons in April 1949, but the pent-up demand of children and the sweet-toothed meant that supplies dried up and rationing was reimposed in August; petrol rationing was finally abandoned in the spring of 1950, as was rationing of a large range of tinned goods. Meat was the last item to go in June 1954 and housewives ceremoniously tore up their ration books in Trafalgar Square, while members of the ever-alert Housewives' League patrolled butcher's shops to check prices, since an increase had been predicted.

While the tentacles of the post-war world lingered, the new decade brought with it a determined effort to 'spring-clean' the old and celebrate the new. The artist John Tunnard, in an interview published in *Vogue* in December 1945, was quoted as saying that his inspiration came 'from the future not the known past or present'.[30] And the future meant science. In 1949 the Festival Pattern Group was set up explicitly to design patterns based on crystal structures, for use in the Festival of Britain in a number of different media – ceramics, glass, textiles, wallpaper, metalwork, furniture, lighting and plastics. The designers were provided with blueprints of the crystal structures of various substances and materials, such as insulin, quartz and polythene, by a scientist from Girton College, Cambridge. Their brief was to use these as inspiration for abstract pattern designs. The initiator of the project, Mark Hartland Thomas, explained that such crystal structures were 'essentially modern because the technique that constructed them was quite recent, and yet, like all successful decoration of the past, they derived from nature – although it was nature at a submicroscopic scale not previously revealed'.[31]

Wallpapers were printed with patterns called 'Insulin' and 'Boric Acid' and a woven textile was produced with a pattern based on the structure of nylon. Nylon was one of the new synthetic materials that came into common use in the early 1950s and revolutionized design in clothing and home decorating. Nylon and Terylene were drip-dry, easy-care fabrics that could be machine-washed and did not need ironing – indeed, Terylene retained a 'permanent' knife crease to trousers and pleated skirts through innumerable washings – and such man-made fabrics could be dyed in vivid, even fluorescent colours. In the home, reinforced fibre-glass enabled the construction of chairs such as Eero Saarinen's 'tulip' chair for Knoll, and Robin Day's stacking chairs, which seemed more like sculpture than furniture, while spindly,

Left
'CONTEMPORARY' TASTE
'Homemaker plate' from a range designed by Enid Seeney for Ridgeway potteries in 1955. Decorated with examples of 'contemporary' design including a boomerang-shaped table and spiky plant holder. The design was mass-produced and found in Woolworth.

Below
ATOMIC FABRIC
Fabric designed for the Festival of Britain in 1951, showing diagrammatic and abstract shapes that owed much to scientific structures.

'Lucky the mother whose table is Formica-topped'

tubular-steel legs on tables and chairs and wire-basket seats made pre-war wooden furniture look dark and bulky.

Floors were covered in geometric thermoplastic floor tiles that were 'easy-wipe'. The plastic laminate Formica had been developed in the 1940s, but it was not until the 1950s that it became the design vernacular that transformed homes and replaced wood and enamelled surfaces, in sheets of patterned plastic simulating woodgrain, or printed with 'Jazz' patterns or the inevitable patterns based on haemoglobin, platelets or amoeba. Again, Formica signalled more than a design revolution: it not only brightened the home, according to its promoters, but lightened women's lives too: 'Lucky the mother whose table is Formica-topped' ran a 1951 advertisement: 'No need to scrub – one wipe with a cloth and it's clean.'[32]

It was hardly surprising that 'science' became the aesthetic of the 1950s. It seemed to promise a new world of discovery – and of control. 'The word science means knowledge,' explained the radio 'Brain's Trust' member, Jacob Bronowski.[33] In 1952 Francis Crick and James Watson (also drawing on the work of Rosalind Franklin) discovered the structure of DNA: three years later a huge helix-shaped chandelier was hung by the furniture shop, Heals, in its stairwell; in 1952 the contraceptive pill was invented; Dr Jonas Salk discovered a vaccination against polio in 1955; it was possible to speak to the US via a transatlantic telephone service in 1956; and a radio telescope was completed at Jodrell Bank in Cheshire in 1957. The sound barrier was broken by a De Havilland 110 jet fighter in 1952 and the conquest of 'outer space' – the prospect of which had proved such a draw in the Dome of Discovery – seemed to be becoming a reality with the launching of two Russian sputniks in 1957 (the stark evidence, if evidence were

needed, that the USSR had cracked the difficulties of Inter-Continental Ballistic Missiles). The Americans did the same a year later and in 1959 the far side of the moon was photographed by Russian luniks.[34]

These advances were reflected in designs like the satellite-shaped Hoover vacuum cleaner and plastic satellite cigarette dispensers, but the preoccupation with space predated its scientific exploration and lay in the fantasy of exploring – and dominating – a new world. *Eagle*, a weekly colour comic for boys started by the Reverend Marcus Morris, first appeared in 1950. Its front page featured the space explorer Captain Dan Dare, 'Pilot of the Future' (it had originally been proposed to call him 'Lex Christian'), who tangled weekly in intergalactic battles with the Mekon, an evil green alien with a huge head.[35] *Eagle* proved immensely popular, though it was expensive at threepence a week, and its

Facing page
A WOMAN'S DOMAIN
After the Second World War women were encouraged by the withdrawal of childcare facilities, unequal wages and working conditions to resume their interrupted roles as homemakers. In the early 1950s the home was portrayed in magazines and advertisements as women's proud fiefdom, a contrast to wartime drudgery and privation.

Above
SCIENTIFIC PROGRESS
Polio had been every parent's nightmare. The discovery of a vaccine in 1955 brought relief, evident in the faces of these mothers queuing with their children at a Middlesex clinic in May 1956.

circulation soon reached a million copies a week, as well as spinning off 'Dan Dare' merchandise like watches, water pistols and lemonade. Dan Dare was the prototype for the 'Hulton's Boys and Girls Exhibition' at Olympia in 1956, which prophesied 'flight in the year 2000'. The jutting-chinned explorer received this accolade because the 'series has, in the past, mirrored with amazing accuracy some of the real-life enterprises which are at present being planned, not only in this country, but in America'.[36] The radio programme *Journey into Space*, which featured a rather more homely – and anxious – space crew, was voted Britain's favourite radio programme in 1954.

But it was not only benign technology that became the cultural vocabulary of the 1950s. In 1945 Japan had been brought to surrender by the explosion of two atomic bombs dropped on Hiroshima and Nagasaki. In August 1949 the USSR successfully tested an atomic bomb – three years earlier than Britain and America had estimated it would be able to.[37] It was not just a space race that was under way: in 1951 the two British scientists who had split the atom twenty years earlier were awarded the Nobel Prize for so doing; the Americans carried out a thermo-nuclear explosion in 1952, and the several-coloured mushroom cloud, twenty-five miles high and a hundred miles wide, 'became the symbol of anxiety for mankind';[38] the same year the first British atomic test was held in the Monte Bello islands in the Pacific; the Russians exploded an H-bomb the following year. Britain's first nuclear power station opened at Calder Hall, Cumbria, in 1956 ; the Russians built a nuclear-powered ship the same year; and an experimental fast reactor began operation at Dounreay in Scotland in 1959.

The 1950s were truly the atomic age and this was reflected in George Nelson's 'atomic clock' of 1949. It consisted of twelve painted wooden knobs radiating on metal spokes, a design that was adapted in myriad ways to produce 'atomic' wastepaper baskets, plant holders, lamps, magazine racks and coat racks – all with 'atoms' on wire structures – and fabrics with patterns based on atomic structures or 'atomic swizzle sticks'.[39]

But the atomic age was more than a design trope: it was the context of the 1950s and beyond. British foreign policy – in recognition both of the end of the dream of a world order based on a superpower, which was dashed at Potsdam in 1945, and of the lost capacity for complete independence – was based on Churchill's concept of the 'three circles' of British influence in the United States, the Commonwealth and Europe. These interlocking and mutually reinforcing circles would provide the foundation for a continuing world role for Britain.[40] But within two years of peace, the circles were wobbling dangerously. On 2 July 1947, the USSR delegation walked out of the Marshall Plan negotiations in Paris, seeing in the proposals for US-assisted European recovery little other than a scheme enabling the US to unload its surplus productive capacity in Europe to bind together a Western capitalist bloc. 'From retail purchase of several European countries Washington has conceived design of wholesale purchase of the whole European continent' was how *Pravda* put it.[41] In response, the USSR tightened its grip on those territories that it controlled in Eastern Europe and replaced the Comintern, which Stalin had disbanded in the wartime years of co-operation, with the Cominform (the Communist Information Bureau). And in 1948 a Russian blockade cut off the British-, American- and French-controlled zones of Berlin. The 'iron curtain dividing Europe', of which Churchill had spoken in Fulton, Missouri, in March 1946, was drawn tight.

Facing page
HOME HELP
In 1948 it was estimated that 40% of Britain's homes connected to the electricity supply had a vacuum cleaner (top), whereas this combined clothes and dishwasher (bottom) demonstrated in August 1946 did not catch on.

Above
COMICS
Thrilling adventures in space – and at boarding school – in full colour photogravure comics, *Eagle* (1950) and the eponymous *Girl* (1951).

In April 1949 the creation of NATO (the North Atlantic Treaty Organization) linked the US, Britain and most of Western Europe (West Germany was not allowed to be a signatory until 1955) in a military alliance, while the Soviet-led Warsaw Pact in the East established a balance of power. That balance was increasingly poised in terms of the nuclear deterrent, which came to be known as Mutually Assured Destruction – or the eponymous MAD.

British involvement during the war in the 'Manhattan Project' to develop the atomic bomb with the US and Canada had left British politicians with the intention of maintaining a nuclear presence after the war. When in 1946 the McMahon Act summarily terminated Anglo-American co-operation in weapons development, it meant that this would become an independent nuclear force. At the time, that did not seem particularly ominous: British defence was primarily tied up with European matters and imperial garrisons – and money was committed to post-war domestic recovery and in particular to Labour's social welfare programme. The Korean War was to change all that.

On the night of 25 June 1950, Communist North Korean troops invaded South Korea across the 38th Parallel, the border agreed by the Soviet Union and the US. A United Nations resolution condemning the action authorized military action, and an ostensibly UN force under US General MacArthur went to the aid of the South. It was a dangerous flashpoint, since both superpower protagonists were recent nuclear powers, and both an escalation in the conflict and the fear that this was a diversion and a dry run for nuclear 'diplomacy' in Europe seemed real and frightening possibilities. The British government recognized that support for the US in Korea was the price it had to pay

Facing page and above
**THE MUSHROOM
CLOUD OF
DESTRUCTION**
Underwater tests of the
US atomic nuclear bomb
at Bikini atoll in the north
Pacific in July 1946: the
silhouettes of the ships
of the 'Guinea Pig' fleet
can be seen in the
vicinity.

Right
FACTS ABOUT THE
BOMB
A pamphlet published by
the government in 1957
as a plain man's guide to
nuclear warfare – to try to
assure the population that
'terrible though the
effects [of the H-bomb]
are, they can be
exaggerated, and the
information given in this
booklet shows that much
could be done to reduce
them and save lives'. But
it admitted that the
prospect was 'grim'.

in the global theatre for the 'special relationship' that recommitted the US to European defence and reconstruction. It established Britain as 'one of the two world powers outside Russia', superior to 'the queue of European nations' that were also in line for American beneficence.[42] It also meant that peace had lasted a little less than five years as khaki battledress was donned again and the weapons of war were reactivated.

The war, which soon involved Mao's China, lasted for three years: it resulted in the loss of 750 British lives, and the heroic stand of the Gloucestershire Regiment in April 1951 has passed into the sad folk memory of war. The Korean War calcified Cold War tensions and led to the escalation of deterrents, as both the US and Russia rushed to outpace their atom bombs with infinitely more powerful hydrogen bombs.

This was an anxious time, with an increasingly powerful and intractable enemy without and, disturbingly, also an enemy within, whose power was hard to estimate, and whose motives seemed to betray not only official secrets but certainties about official competence and clear boundaries of loyalty and trust. In 1950, Dr Klaus Fuchs, head of theoretical physics at the Atomic Energy Research Establishment at Harwell, was arrested after a tip-off from the FBI. Fuchs had worked on the atom-bomb project at Los Alamos. At his Old Bailey trial he was unequivocal: 'When I learned the purpose of my work, I decided to inform Russia... I had no hesitation in giving all the information I had.'[43] Fuchs was sentenced to fourteen years' imprisonment; 'all the information' could have saved the USSR ten years' worth of research.

On 25 May 1951, two British diplomats left Britain on the night ferry bound for Saint-Malo in Brittany. Guy Burgess and Donald Maclean were en route to Moscow.

Maclean had spent most of the war and after at the British Embassy in Washington, where he had had unlimited access to the classified material on nuclear fission at the HQ of the Atomic Energy Research Establishment, which he was known to visit late at night. He was a very heavy drinker, as was his fellow-diplomat Guy Burgess, who had worked for MI5 and MI6 at various points during the war and who joined Maclean in Washington under the wing of 'Kim' Philby, the First Secretary, who was also covertly working for MI6 and promised to keep an eye on him. Their impeccable background – public school, Cambridge, the Foreign Office, friends of talent in high places – seems to have counted for more than Burgess' and Maclean's sexual indiscretions (Burgess was a priapic homosexual and Maclean a womanizer), drunkenness and general unreliability and in 1950 Maclean was recalled to London to take up the post of

Above
THE THIRD MAN
The 1949 top box office British 'film noir', written by Graham Greene, directed by Carol Reed and starring Orson Welles as Harry Lime. This film of intrigue and mistrust in war-ravaged, occupied Vienna, was the last of the post-war 'spiv' films (though this black market was in dilute penicillin) which has also been seen as the first of the Cold War films.

head of the US department at the Foreign Office. By early 1951, official complaints about Burgess' behaviour led to his own recall to London, where he was able to warn Maclean that the net was closing: evidence of a haemorrhage of information to Russia during the war pointed increasingly to Maclean. The two spies defected. The US authorities suspected that Philby was the 'Third Man' who had warned Burgess and Maclean, but he was cleared by a Parliamentary inquiry. In 1963 Philby also defected to Moscow.

Harold Nicolson commented on the Burgess and Maclean affair: 'I mind dreadfully. (1) Because it shames my dear old profession; (2) because it will enrage the Americans; (3) because it will make everyone suspicious of quite innocent people; (4) because I fear poor Guy will be rendered very unhappy in the end. If he has done a bunk to Russia, they will only use him for a month or so, and then shove him quietly into some salt-mine.'[44] In 1954 a Russian defector told the Western press that Burgess and Maclean had been spying for the USSR since they had been undergraduates at Cambridge. A government White Paper on the affair did little to assuage the feeling of 'an incurable disposition to doubt and suspect all impeccable authorities [in England]'.[45] Indeed, it was in an article about Burgess and Maclean, published in the *Spectator* in September 1953, that the political commentator Henry Fairlie first used the words 'the Establishment' (which, he charged, had closed ranks to protect the spies) to describe that amalgam of those at the top in politics, the administration and the Church who are 'a priori right'. It was a phrase that would soon become common currency.

There were to be several more major global confrontations between the Communist powers in Europe and the Far East

and the US and Europe: the Soviet suppression of the Hungarian uprising in 1956; the Suez crisis the same year; the Cuban missile crisis in 1962; the war in Vietnam from 1964 to 1975 – all of which put into focus Britain's role in the world and her 'special relationship' with the US – before a gradual thaw in Cold War relations and the slow and uneven growth of a period of *détente* starting in the 1970s.

The Korean War – like the later conflicts – had a significant impact on domestic British politics. In 1950 the Ministry of Defence had great difficulty in assembling a combat-ready brigade out of an army of 400,000 men. Richard Hoggart, a member of the reserve forces called up for a fortnight's refresher training, recalls, 'Almost all of us looked much as we had when we were demobbed, but a little fuller in the cheeks and generally softer in our lines and expressions. We also looked and felt – and proved – extremely cack-handed in our gun drills, both officers and men… We were in some ways professionally refreshed in the two weeks, but I doubt if the North Koreans, or, later, the Chinese would have noticed. The most astonishing aspect of the whole enterprise was the sight of our guns and gear. In all important respects they were those on which we had trained in the early Forties, and dragged through the war. No magnificent and sophisticated new electronics from the arms industry in the intervening years. Standing on those bleak Welsh coastal hills, shouting old orders, time was collapsed. This could have been Llandrindod Wells, or…the Tunisian desert….or…Naples.'[46] The 1947 National Service Act reintroduced wartime conscription for all men over eighteen for one year. In December 1948 the period was extended to eighteen months and, in the months after the outbreak of the Korean War, to two years, and this continued for another ten years. It was, Attlee maintained, 'a reasonable thing for the state to ask in return for the welfare state'.[47] But to the 160,000 or so young men who were called up annually, it seemed a waste of two years of their young lives – 'a lot of time is wasted in the army just hanging around'.[48] In some cases it meant foreign travel – to Germany or military hot-spots like Korea, Malaya or Cyprus – and it invariably meant sexual education and experimentation, and often the postponement or disruption of education, training or apprenticeships. The feeling of regimentation for no certain purpose probably fertilized the anarchism that was to be more evident in the next decade, rather than the obedience, short hair and patriotic deference that National Service was supposed to instil (according to those critics who regretted its ending, and on occasion still call for its return).

The Attlee government, which had prioritized domestic reconstruction, embarked on a crash rearmament programme. The aim was to build up, over three years, an army of ten divisions with large reserves, to strengthen the Navy and the RAF and speed up the re-equipment of all three services. The effect on the country's convalescent economy was traumatic. Expenditure on defence almost doubled and in 1952 accounted for 11 per cent of GNP (gross national product) – the highest of any country other than the Soviet Union. The balance of payments, which had run at a satisfactory surplus of £307 million in 1950, plunged into a deficit of £700 million in 1951.[49] There were politicians and economists then, and historians now, who maintain that this was too high a price to pay; that Britain's rearmament programme was unnecessarily ambitious (the Conservative government scaled it down when it took office) and was undertaken to ensure a US commitment to Europe; and that, in undertaking it, the British 'economic miracle' that was poised to happen in 1951 went off track – affluence was postponed.[50]

It certainly had an effect on politics: the Labour Chancellor, Hugh Gaitskell, was convinced that the only place where savings could be made in his 1951 budget was in the social services in general, and the National Health Service in particular. His proposal was to save £13 million by imposing charges on spectacles and dentures, which had previously been free. The Health Secretary, Nye Bevan, convinced that the Soviet threat was always exaggerated and unshakeably opposed to any erosion in the principle of a free health service, resigned, as did Harold Wilson. 'It is really a fight for the soul of the Labour Party,' Gaitskell recognized.[51] It was a fight that was fought out of office for thirteen years over issues of public ownership and nuclear power, when the Bevan who had fought for a nuclear deterrent for Britain that was independent of US weapons policy, led his followers in opposition to the further development of a hydrogen bomb in 1955.

In November 1955, Harold Macmillan insisted that 'we must rely on the power of the nuclear deterrent, or we must throw in the sponge',[52] and in the aftermath of Britain's humiliating withdrawal from Suez in December 1956, there were urgent reasons to question the efficiency of conventional British forces, since, despite the large sums spent on defence since 1950, it had taken nearly three months to organize the British expeditionary force to Egypt; and the suppression by Soviet tanks of the Hungarian uprising had shown that Russia's grip on Eastern Europe remained total and aggressive in defence of the Soviet power bloc. A government White Paper in April 1957, the same month that Britain successfully tested the air-dropped H-bomb, firmly committed the nation to a strategy of 'massive nuclear retaliation', even in the event of a conventional Soviet attack on the West.

Above
'YOU'RE IN THE ARMY NOW'
Military conscription, known as National Service, was reintroduced in 1947 for all males between 18 and 26. A new recruit arrives at a Scots Guards depot, soon to exchange his civilian clothes for a khaki soldier's kit.

Left
BASIC TRAINING
National Servicemen in the Welsh Guards undergoing physical exercises that will make soldiers of them.

The White Paper 'frankly recognized that there is at present no means of providing adequate protection for the people of this country against the consequences of an attack with nuclear weapons'.[53] In March 1948 workmen had begun to demolish the air-raid shelters in Lincoln's Inn: the very next day, the then Home Secretary, Sir John Anderson, recommended that the government should start building new shelters – as protection against the atom bomb.[54] The construction of Thor missile bases was planned for East Anglia; there were frequent reports of RAF and US Air Force bomber patrols flying over Britain; and the vulnerability of a people already alarmed by reports of the effects of radiation in the atmosphere, as a result of nuclear tests, seemed very real.[55] At the Labour Party Conference in Brighton in October 1957, Nye Bevan came out in favour of Britain maintaining an independent nuclear deterrent, since to renounce it would mean that 'you will send a Foreign Secretary, whoever he may be, naked into the conference chamber'. The last hope of political action seemed lost: anxieties about nuclear power – coupled with strong opposition, particularly among the young, to the apparent last gasp of British gunboat diplomacy over Suez – meant that an article by J.B. Priestley published in the New Statesman at the end of 1957, calling for Britain to take a moral lead in the world by contracting out of the nuclear arms race, found an enthusiastic response.[56]

At the end of January 1958, a wartime RAF chaplain, Canon Collins of St Paul's Cathedral, held a press conference to announce the formation of the Campaign for Nuclear Disarmament, the aim of which was 'to channel the existing emotion in the country and create a climate of opinion which would make it essential for the political parties to follow'.[57] Collins was to be CND's chairman and the philosopher, Bertrand Russell, its president. At the first meeting in

February 1958, 5,000 people flocked to Westminster Hall, despite the fact that the publicity had been minimal.[58] The historian A.J.P. Taylor described the effects of an H-bomb explosion. 'Is there anyone here who would want to do this to another human being?' he asked. There was silence in the hall. 'Then why are we making the damned thing?' he demanded. The movement was born and on Good Friday that year hundreds gathered in Trafalgar Square to march the fifty miles to the atomic research establishment at Aldermaston in Berkshire, singing 'Ban, ban, ban, the bloody H-bomb' and their own version of 'When the Saints Go Marching In'.[59] 'The weather was grim,' wrote Jeff Nutall, who was there. 'Trad jazz floated out over the sodden Berkshire fields. When they got to the austere secretive place of concrete, barbed wire and little civic lavatories, they didn't walk in and smash it up, as some more realistic marchers had hoped, but they did discover that they were not alone. The march had gathered numbers impressively [there were an estimated 8,000 by the end of that first march]. After all the snarling and planning in shuttered rooms, the public response was deliriously encouraging.'[60]

CND had a political aim: that of persuading the government to sign up to its slogan to 'Ban the Bomb', but the majority of those thousands who joined CND and took part in the Easter march (which after the first year culminated in a massive rally in Trafalgar Square, the traditional home of radical protest) were not members of the Labour Party, or of any other party. To them it was a moral crusade: a commentary on the seemingly selfish and hidebound society of affluent 1950s' Britain. As Priestley had said in his clarion call: 'the British of these times, so frequently hiding their decent, kind faces behind masks of sullen apathy or sour, cheap cynicism, often seem to be waiting for

Facing page
THE FASTEST MAN IN BRITAIN
Roger Bannister, a 25-year-old medical student, breasts the tape after running a mile in 3 minutes 59.4 seconds at the Oxford University running track, 6 May 1954.

Left
CND
A poster advertising the 1959 Easter march to ban the bomb, showing the distinctive logo of the Campaign for Nuclear Disarmament.

Below
ALDERMASTON MARCH
The 1960 march with Canon Collins and Jacquetta Hawkes in the vanguard. 'The H-bomb is the supreme moral issue of the day', Collins told the first CND gathering.

michael foot

In October 1957 Michael Foot [leader of the Labour Party in the '80s] penned an article for *Tribune*. Under the headline 'Bevan and the Bomb', it was a response to Aneurin Bevan's speech at the Labour Party Conference that year in which he argued that a unilateralist Britain that did not have an independent nuclear weapon would have no diplomatic leverage in disarmament talks. Foot put the counter case in his article: 'It would be hypocritical to surrender our own bomb and merely be content to shelter behind someone else's. But it would not be immoral to abandon our own bomb and seek the best diplomatic means we have to ensure that others did the same. The power of example might be one of the best ways of securing that end...I am convinced a growing number of people throughout the country will believe that Britain's readiness to renounce the weapon which we all regard as an invention of the devil could capture the imagination of millions of people in many lands'.[61]

It was a rallying cry and a campaign that Michael Foot was to spearhead through CND for the decades to come.

Facing page and above
MARCHING TO BAN
THE BOMB
'CND...provoked furious enthusiasms and enmities, and made a spectacular appeal particularly to the young, precisely because it did not take refuge in vague generalities, precisely because it did urge that something could be done'.

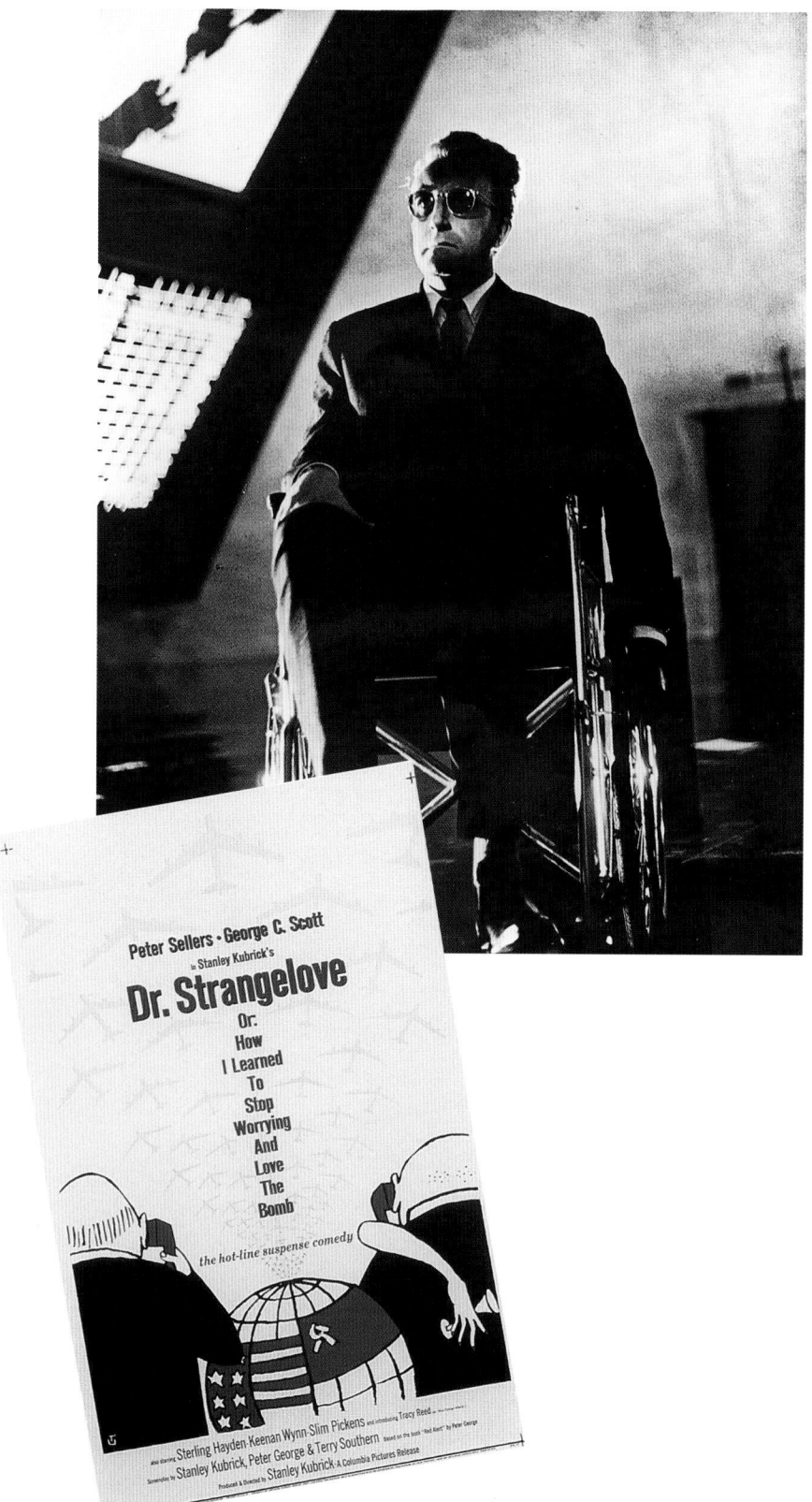

something better than party squabbles and appeals to their narrowest self-interest, something great and noble in its intention that would make them feel good again'.[62]

To Jeff Nutall it was a 'spiritual hunger march' and he felt, as he trooped through what the marchers dubbed 'Radioactive country', that it was 'above all a civilizing mission, a march away from fear towards normality…a gathering point for the population who wanted to express their disturbance, to comfort themselves that there were perhaps enough people of like mind to be politically effective, to test the potency of their anxieties and ideals in the democracy, and above all to reinstate common decency as the condition of man.'[63]

It was a new departure: 'official circles are confused and alarmed about the Campaign for Nuclear Disarmament,' the *New Statesman* (admittedly a partisan supporter) reported in 1958, 'because it is a movement of a new pattern. It is unprecedented because it has no political group behind it; no showman's drum beats it up; it has no leaders serving personal ambitions; it is not inspired or indeed supported by the Communist Party, which is embarrassed by the obvious retort that the Soviet Union should also abandon nuclear weapons.'[64] But eventually the Campaign would have to tackle party politics and that would split the movement in the early 1960s.

CND attracted largely middle-class supporters – those same 'herbivores' who, in Michael Frayn's view, were behind the Festival of Britain – although when a CND motion calling for unilateral disarmament succeeded at the 1960 Labour Party Conference, it was primarily thanks to the trade-union block-vote. Alan Brien, writing in the *Daily Mail*, characterized the marchers as 'the sort of people who would normally spend Easter listening to a Beethoven concert on the Home Service [now Radio Four], pouring dry sherry from a decanter for the neighbours, painting a Picasso design on hard-boiled eggs, attempting the literary competitions in the weekly papers, or going to church with the children. Instead they were walking through the streets in their old clothes.'[65] It seemed at times in the words of the historian A.J.P. Taylor, who continued to be an active supporter, a 'movement of eggheads for eggheads',[66] including John Berger, Michael Tippett, Philip Toynbee, Peggy Ashcroft, Doris Lessing, John Osborne, Kenneth Tynan, George Melly and Arnold Wesker.[67]

However, the protest predominantly attracted the young and gave them a feeling of active participation in the affairs of their country, from which they had so long felt excluded and unrecognized. 'They made each march a carnival of optimism…protest was associated with festivity'.[68] There were active university branches of CND from the beginning, and in 1962 the *Guardian* estimated that only about one in twenty of those on the Aldermaston march was over the age of twenty, and many were under eighteen. With their duffel coats, black sweaters, long hair, beards, banners, folk songs, jazz bands and skiffle music, the protesters were easy game for the press, which found it hard to come to terms with the fact that in 1961 100,000 people packed into Trafalgar Square to affirm their opposition to a nuclear threat that would escalate frighteningly the next year with the Cuban missile crisis.

In the early 1960s the movement was split by those who called for direct action – and got arrested in their hundreds when they attempted civil disobedience[69] – and those who saw that the route to disarmament lay through political persuasion. The signing of a partial nuclear test-ban treaty in July 1963 and the closing of Labour ranks to fight – and win – the 1964 election, drained CND of much of its support, but its existence had demonstrated the appeal of the British tradition of radical protest and had recognized the emergence of that late 1950s' phenomenon: the teenager who was no longer in transition between childhood and adulthood, but was a sentient being of whom account would have to be taken – one day by politicians, but already by the producers of goods and culture, who recognized that the designation 'teenager' was now a market category, rather than simply a chronological description.

Facing page
'DR. STRANGELOVE OR, HOW I LEARNED TO STOP WORRYING AND LOVE THE BOMB' Stanley Kubrick's 1963 black comedy in which Peter Sellers (top) played three roles: the US president, an RAF officer, and a mad scientist. The story about a crazed US general's paranoia about 'commies' – and women – leads to nuclear wipe out, was powerful propaganda against nuclear weapons.

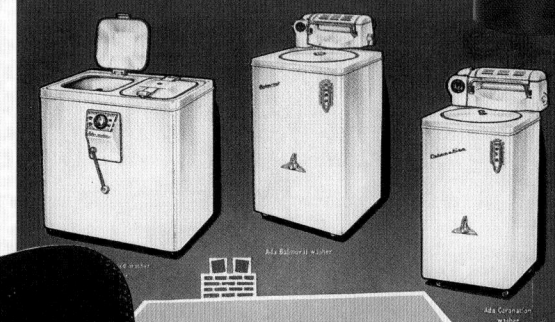

affluence

'Money doesn't chink these days; it crackles louder than a forest fire'

Above
'YOUR'E LOOKING AT A
CONSERVATIVE' (1950s
ADVERTISING SLOGAN)
The Prime Minister,
Harold Macmillan,
shooting grouse on the
Yorkshire Moors on 15
August 1957, the year the
Conservative Party
started planning for the
1959 General Election.
Confident in the buoyant
economy, the party
advertisements
proclaimed 'You've had it
good. Have it Better, Vote
Conservative'. Millions
did: the Tories were
returned with an
increased majority of 107
seats over Labour.

'When did you last hear the word austerity?' asked *Queen* magazine in 1959. 'This is the only time you will see it in this issue. At the moment there is more money in Britain than ever before. Nearly two thousand million pounds is pouring out of pockets and wallets and handbags [and *Queen* featured a gold mesh one costing 5 guineas from Jarrolds to illustrate their point] and changing into air tickets and oysters, television sets and caviar, art treasures and vacuum cleaners, cigars and refrigerators. Britain has launched into an age of unparalleled lavish living. It came unobtrusively. But now you are living in a new world... Money doesn't chink these days; it crackles louder than a forest fire. It is the age of BOOM.'[1]

It certainly was not like that for everyone of course. The working title for J.K. Galbraith's influential book *The Age of Affluence*, published the previous year, had been Why People Are Poor. 'As I dealt with the conditions and consequences of affluence under which the existence of the poor had been buried, the poverty I had set out to write about got pushed further and further towards the back of the book,' he explained. 'A lot of people never read that far.'[2] It had not been like that for very long, but the years from 1955 to 1964 had attracted 'affluence' as a prefix, just as its polar opposite 'austerity' had encompassed the previous decade. It was as though the social revolution that 1945 heralded had taken ten years to work through in economic terms – a decade when the promise of prosperity seemed always postponed; when Britain's skyline remained almost unchanged, with the devastation of war still apparent; when newspapers were limited by the availability of newsprint; when the BBC controlled the airwaves; and when Britain's banks were 'driving a very powerful car at twenty miles an hour'.[3]

When Churchill had been returned to office in 1951, the Conservatives' election slogan had been 'Set the people free' – from ration books, identity cards, building licences, restriction on credit and shortage of goods. Britain was still hampered with the costs of post-war reconstruction and – in no small part as a result of the Korean War, and all that this suggested about the realities of power in the post-war world – committed to an unsustainably high defence budget that absorbed almost 30 per cent of government spending.[4]

But slowly the economy recovered and in the latter half of the 1950s incomes rose as taxes fell. In 1950 the average wage had been £6. 8s.; by 1959 it had almost doubled to £11. 2s. 6d.; the standard rate of income tax, which had been 9s. 6d. in the pound in 1951, had fallen to 7s. 9d. by 1959; and the level of income on which surtax was levied rose in 1961 from £2,000 a year to £5,000. Full employment was almost achieved: between 1948 and 1970 the number of registered unemployed averaged just 2 per cent in only eight of those twenty-three years. On 20 July 1957, Macmillan, Prime Minister since Eden's resignation in the wake of the Suez crisis the previous year, gave a speech at Bedford: 'Indeed,' he said, 'let us be frank about it: most of our people have never had it so good. Go round the country, go to the industrial towns, go to the farms and you will see a prosperity such as we have never had in my life-time – nor indeed in the history of the country.'[5] It was a speech that was to resonate for the rest of Macmillan's political career and beyond, and it was not long before it would seem a hollow and selfish sentiment, but at the time it reported on a reality. Though there were already ominous signs: the 'pound in your pocket' had lost one-third of its value in the years from 1950 to 1959, and while British productivity had grown by 40 per cent, that of Germany and Italy had risen by 150 per cent and of Japan by 400 per cent.

Above
HIGH-RISING LONDON
'A twentieth-century solution' which introduced 'some badly needed variety to the London skyline'. The *Architect's Journal*'s verdict in November 1959 on the new Castrol House in Marylebone, London.

JAMES DEAN is my real name.
Height? 5 feet 10 inches . . .
Weight? 155 pounds . . . *Colour of
eyes?* Blue . . . *Hair?* Blond . . .
Nationality? American . . . *Where were
you born?* Fairmount, Indiana . . . *Date
of Birth?* February 8, 1931. . . .
What schools did you attend? Grammar
and High School in Fairmount.
College? University of California at
Los Angeles.
In what school sports did you participate?
Baseball, track, basketball. *Did you take
part in school dramatics?* Yes.
*Were any of your relatives theatrical
people?* No.
Who brought you up? My uncle and
aunt, as my mother died while I was a
baby.
When did you start acting? In High
School.
*To whom do you give credit for stimulating
your interest in acting?* To James Whitmore,

Housing, which remained the number-one post-war priority, was the platform of the Tory victory in 1951: their ministers accused Bevan, who combined Health and Housing in a joint ministry, of keeping 'only half an Nye'[6] on housing in his preoccupation with the introduction of the National Health Service. With a priority of industrial reconstruction to aid the export drive, the number of houses built had now fallen from 250,000 a year to 200,000 for the previous three years. The Conservatives pledged to do better than that. Harold Macmillan recalled, 'Winston [Churchill] asked me if I could build 300,000 houses in a year and if so I could be Minister of Housing. I agreed on condition I could run it my way. We ran it, in fact, like a war department... I'd learnt a thing or two working at the Ministry of Supply working with tycoons.'[7] The target was reached in 1953 and was sustained for the next five years – though the high standard of council housing insisted on by Bevan was scaled down, and the mid-1950s saw the explosion of 'vertical villages': tower blocks that dominated the urban landscape.

The 'modern movement' among architects drew inspiration for its ferro-concrete constructions of the 1950s and 1960s from the work of the French architect Le Corbusier. His *Unité d'Habitation* in Marseilles from 1947–52, was the size of a large village – or suburb – and housed 1,600 people in some 300 units of accommodation, mostly flats. There were two floors of shops, a restaurant, a doctor's surgery, a crèche and spare rooms for guests, all arranged along interior 'streets', with a playground and an athletic track on the roof. The whole edifice floated on 'piloti' – two-storey-high, vast concrete stilts that made the buildings' self-contained sufficiency appear total.

Such a 'brutalist' construction seemed breathtakingly 'honest' in its undisguised, unsmoothed screeds of poured concrete slabs – and the answer to the housing shortage and the need to rebuild office accommodation for an expanding population of civil servants, administrators and businesses, as cheaply and quickly as possible in prime city sites.

With a housing shortage of dispiriting proportions, the pioneering London County Council led the way to a Le Corbusier-inspired 'total community' in the sky, with the Alton estate in Roehampton, south-west London, started in 1952 and finished four years later. Here the eleven-storey blocks soared 100 feet high on concrete trunks similar to those used in Marseilles. The rents were not cheap and many of the rehoused tenants came to miss the tight-knit communities they had left in the East End; they felt 'boxed in' and isolated in their flats, which saw no passing traffic, and the camaraderie of the mean streets they had known seemed to have vanished. But at first the modernity – 'partial central heating', fitted kitchens and such concepts as dining alcoves and 'breakfast bars', all designed to get the maximum living into the minimum space – plus the sense of fresh air and panoramic vistas glimpsed from aluminium-framed windows seemed compensation enough.[8]

Soon tower blocks of prefabricated concrete were going up in all the major cities – Birmingham, Coventry, Plymouth, Manchester, Glasgow – where bombs had fallen, or where pre-war housing was by now so dilapidated that the conversion of gas mantles to electricity and the addition of a bathroom (to replace the weekly tin tub in front of the fire, or a visit to the public baths) and an inside toilet (to replace the outside privy or WC shared by several families, plus the chamber pots under beds) represented insufficient upgrade for post-war standards of human habitation.

But there was a vision as well as a necessity to it all: Sir Hugh Casson, who had been the architect in charge of the

Your food spread about you.

Facing page
REBEL WITHOUT A CAUSE
A 'crazy mixed-up kid', the delinquent hero from across the Atlantic who lived fast and died young (in a car crash aged 24), James Dean, the star of *Rebel Without a Cause* (1955) gave British youth an image of teenage rebellion and alienation.

Below
THE JOYS OF INDEPENDENCE
Ronald Searle's view of bedsitter life from *London – So Help Me*, by Winifred Ellis.

Above
THE L-SHAPED ROOM
A 1962 film directed by
Bryan Forbes from Lynne
Reid Bank's novel (1960)
about a range of '50s
characters living in
Notting Hill bedsits – an
unmarried pregnant girl
(Leslie Caron), a tyro
writer (Tom Bell), a gay
Black man (Brock Peters),
a seedy landlord, and a
tart with a heart.

Festival of Britain, was also part of the team that designed Stevenage new town. 'The war and the restrictions on building had frustrated architects for ten years. Young architects in their thirties had had the chance to build nothing but huts and hangars. Half of them went into public service for local authorities with the idealistic belief that planning and organization could solve any social problem…the high-rise cluster was part of the ethos of the time. The social problems such as neurosis and vandalism were ignored.'[9]

As well as pushing ahead with local-authority housing, the private sector was expanding fast: 60 per cent of all British housing was accommodation rented from private landlords at the beginning of the 1950s and rents were frozen at 1939 prices. The 1957 Rent Act allowed landlords to charge what they could get for all new (that is, vacated) accommodation and for all property with a high rateable value, while other rents could be increased. The result was to free up some private rented accommodation and to encourage landlords that it was worth taking in tenants. It was also an incentive for unscrupulous landlords to pressurize – or terrorize – tenants in controlled-rent accommodation to leave, so that the rent could be substantially raised. The early 1960s coined a word for this practice – 'Rachmanism' – after a particularly odious Paddington landlord. The Act also worked as an incentive to make sure that accommodation was 'furnished', since it then fell outside the provision of the Act and tenants could be evicted at a week's notice (though there was a degree of slow legal redress through rent tribunals). 'Furnished' could simply mean having a bed, a table and chairs and a wardrobe, and led to a situation where living out of a suitcase became a way of life.

The rented sector in cities catered for a wide range of people: on the one hand, young professionals – named by the media as 'bachelors' and 'bachelor girls' – who either lived in 'digs', with a landlady providing meals and laundry (this form of accommodation was more popular with men), or in bedsitters or shared flats where you did your own cooking and laundry (women tended to prefer these).[10] This spoke to a changing society, with the growth of commercial, service and media jobs in the cities and single young people prepared to leave home before marriage – and earning just about enough to do so. A Flatsharers' Register was set up in 1958 to cater for 'those who face the ordeal of coming to London for the first time'.[11] It was inundated – by more women than men, women who saw delights in the 'independence' of a shared ironing board, lines of stockings drying over the bath and a voracious gas meter.

These 'bachelor' people with their disposable income and 'lifestyle' aspirations were beloved of women's magazines, which were adept at advising how to make your L-shaped room seem 'gay' (a very 1950s' word), with 'individual touches' in rooms where the furniture was not yours and you were not allowed to decorate – by adding 'a pretty lampshade'; by throwing a bright piece of fabric (when 'throw' in decorating terms was still a verb); by 'pushing the bookcase up against the bed to make a headboard'; by buying or making a wool rug in a 'contemporary' design. And, if you were not allowed either to paint or hang floral wallpaper, or even accent your alcoves, then 'hang a large piece of fabric or wallpaper, school map fashion, from the picture rail'.[12]

At the other end of the market were those who had neither the necessary points to get a council house or flat, nor sufficient capital to buy a home of their own. Among these

Above
IMMIGRATION
Haywood Magee's photograph for *Picture Post* in June 1956 of 'West Indian immigrants' at Victoria Station. The story was headlined 'Thirty Thousand Colour Problems'. The first problem for the newly-arrived immigrants – mainly from Jamaica and mainly men at this time – was the cold, but problems of housing, jobs, discrimination and racism were not far behind.

Above
A BRIGHT FUTURE
An advertisement for fitted
carpets and advice on the
'confusing range of
boarding' from the
February 1960 issue of
Good Housekeeping, and
one from the *Architects
Journal* for new materials,
tough vinyl tiles for
corporate settings.

were the 'new Britons', immigrants from the British colonies,
wartime fighters, who had started to come to Britain in 1947
largely from the West Indies in response to the demand for
skilled labour, whose numbers had reached nearly 30,000 by
1956 – hardly an influx – and for whom housing was usually
a nightmare of discrimination and exploitation. 'No
coloureds' was a frequent coda to any newspaper small ad or
postcard in a newsagent's window offering accommodation
– and sometimes it added 'no Irish, no children and no dogs'
to show the catholicity of British prejudice. If there was no
such disclaimer, then a man, or family, newly arrived from
Jamaica or Trinidad was invariably told 'It's already let' when
they turned up to view. If they did find somewhere to live,
the 'black tax' was the price that the immigrants with no
capital (and no foot on the local authority's housing ladder)
paid for accommodation that could only have been let to
white people at half the rent that was demanded from those
disparagingly called 'darkies'.

The Conservative Party saw that the surest way of
fulfilling its popular Disraelian mission was to turn Britain
into a 'property-owning democracy', and to ensure this took
place, more than half the new houses built between 1955
and 1964 were owner-occupied, and in 1963 owner-
occupiers were given a tax boost too.[13]

If it made no sense for those in rented accommodation to
decorate or buy furniture, then the new home-owners were
in an altogether different position. Having saved hard to
scrimp a deposit and calculate the mortgage repayments,
they might not have been able to go out and furnish from
scratch straight away, but equally most were determined that
a new home meant a new style. During the 1950s spending
on household items increased by 115 per cent.[14] But
what sort of style was it?

In 1952 the Design and Industries Association mounted an exhibition at Charing Cross Station called 'Register Your Choice', in an attempt to find out what the British wanted in their homes, so that the recovering domestic manufacturing industries could get it right. The result was surprising: three out of five opted for choice 'R' – the modern room with its angular lights and its fashionable splay-legged furniture. What they liked was the 'gaiety of its colours' and the 'simplicity' of the furniture, which created an airy, spacious feeling and promised minimal housework to keep it so. If the results of the survey were surprising, they were also misleading. A Mass-Observation survey polled at the same time revealed that those voting were an unrepresentative sample of the population; anyway, it was one thing to admire 'contemporary design', and quite another to buy it. When it came to shelling out hard-earned money, room L – the traditional room, all rounded, plump lines, frills, fringes and 'details' – won hands down.[15] It was for living in, not looking at; anyway it would go with the wedding-present rug and the hand-me-down sideboard, in a way that the purity of the 'arty', 'Scandinavian' look would not.

On the whole it was younger people who had preferred the 'contemporary' look and, with new homes being built to tighter specifications and with multi-purpose rooms, traditional, heavy furniture looked bulky, took up too much room and was irritatingly mono-purpose. 'Non-unit' furniture came to replace the three-piece suite; fitted units took over from glass cabinets; and the back-to-the-wall sideboards of old were now replaced by janus-like units that could divide a room and be filled from either side.

In textiles and carpets, floral was out, and abstract swirls, geometric patterns and 'folk weave' fabrics were all the rage. And with the gradual adoption of central heating and the end

Above
WIPE DOWN
MODERNITY
An advertisement in
Architect's Journal (1959)
for the 'materials of today'.

Left
MODERN COMFORT
Ernest Race's
contemporary version of
the wing chair.

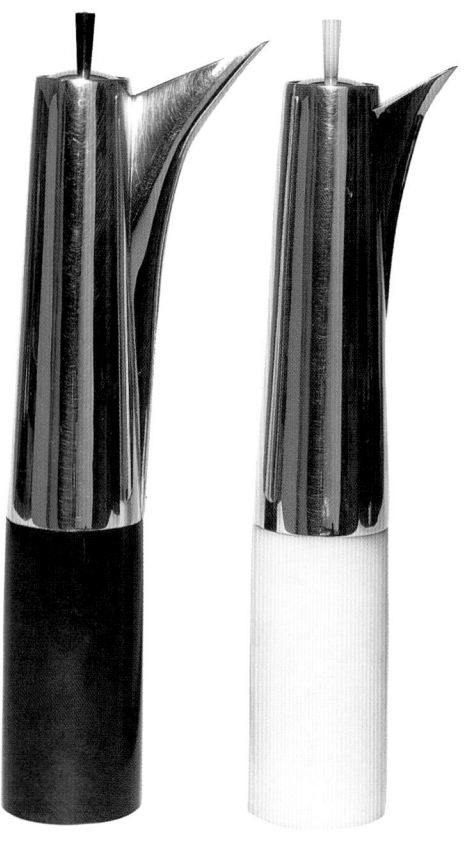

of coal fires – and either the failure to build, or the removal
of, the traditional clock-and-two-symmetrical-ornaments-
mantelpiece – the focal point of a room seemed to be up for
grabs, for a time.

The problem was, as always, that 'good design', as decreed
by the Council of Industrial Design, by architects and
designers and as promoted by the more up-market home
magazines (though in 1952 the editor of the mass-circulation
Woman magazine was invited to sit on the committee of the
COID), was dependent on it being available to consumers –
and on the consumers knowing that they wanted it. The
Festival of Britain had seemed a beacon on this highway, but
shortage of mass production and money in the early 1950s
had frustrated that. Only a few shops, mainly in London,
were promoting contemporary furniture – the most
noticeable being Heals, although there were a few others,

including an imaginative furniture-sales person with a design
mission at John Lewis; she used to write out orders for
fictitious customers, who would then 'cancel' their order just
as the furniture arrived, so that it had to be displayed in the
shop – that, she hoped, would stimulate orders from real
customers.[16] Most furniture retailers in the 1950s were
convinced that they just knew what their public wanted,
even if they were only prepared to show them what they
already knew about. It was an economy – and an aesthetic –
of the repeat order.

In the department of household appliances, it was a
different story. Women who had worked at two jobs
during wartime, often spending long hours in a munitions
factory or taking the place of a man who had been called up
for active service, then working as hard again queuing for up
to two hours a day for the family's necessities (and 'making

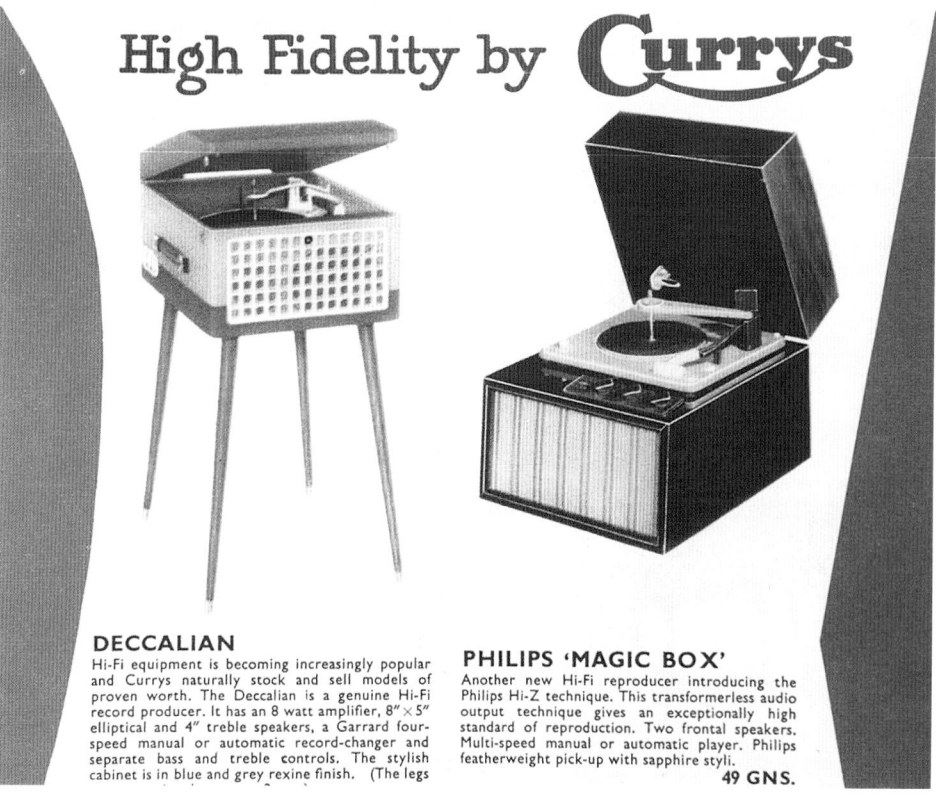

High Fidelity by Currys

DECCALIAN
Hi-Fi equipment is becoming increasingly popular and Currys naturally stock and sell models of proven worth. The Deccalian is a genuine Hi-Fi record producer. It has an 8 watt amplifier, 8″ × 5″ elliptical and 4″ treble speakers, a Garrard four-speed manual or automatic record-changer and separate bass and treble controls. The stylish cabinet is in blue and grey rexine finish. (The legs

PHILIPS 'MAGIC BOX'
Another new Hi-Fi reproducer introducing the Philips Hi-Z technique. This transformerless audio output technique gives an exceptionally high standard of reproduction. Two frontal speakers. Multi-speed manual or automatic player. Philips featherweight pick-up with sapphire styli.
49 GNS.

do' with what she managed to get), were suddenly no longer wanted in the workplace. 'Housewife' had to be seen as a role to aspire to, but it must not replicate the pre-war drudgery; and yet, for those who had them before the war, servants were now largely a thing of the past and a twice-weekly 'char' was the most for which the majority of middle-class women could hope.

By the time they were twenty-five, almost three-quarters of English girls were married, a number of them having negotiated 'necking' and even 'heavy petting' sessions, so that they still walked up the aisle as virgins in white. 'The high value put on virginity for both sexes is remarkable, and I should suspect, specifically English,' reflected the author Geoffrey Gorer, who had investigated attitudes towards sex in 1950.[17] His questionnaire revealed that 55 per cent of men and 73 per cent of women disapproved of women having

sexual experience before marriage (though, perhaps equally characteristically, only 50 per cent disapproved of it for men). The predictable post-war 'baby bulge' had taken longer to subside than anyone had predicted and, armed with copies of Dr Spock's *Baby and Child Care* (first published in Britain in 1955, and eventually selling 20 million copies worldwide), and aware of, if not armed, with John Bowlby's *Child Care and the Growth of Love* (which came out in 1953), mothers who could afford it could be convinced of the value – and full-time occupation, with all that constant attention and activity – of rearing the next generation.

The boom in consumer goods in the 1950s constructed the woman, the home-maker, as the linchpin of this new 'people's capitalism', and to the advertiser she was an object of attention to be wooed with ardour. Being a housewife was portrayed by relentless advertising as an immensely

Above
MODERN DESIGN, MODERN BEAT
Two 'hi-fi' record players from Curry's, so named because of the true sound reproduction they claimed to achieve as they spun 78 and 33 rpm records with a fragile plastic stylus keeping the needle in the groove. Most households – and certainly every teenager – longed for such a 'magic box' in the '50s.

desirable state, a matter of pretty pinnies, a 'labour-saving', gadget-filled home, and grateful and well-groomed husbands, appreciative of the efforts of the wife, who seemed to have all the attributes of a permanent hostess. Addressing the Advertising Conference in 1957, Mary Grieve, the editor of *Woman*, made the point: 'In her function as a consumer, an immense amount of a woman's personality is engaged. Success here is as vitalizing to her as success in his chosen sphere to a man.'[18]

'I love my New English Refrigerator,' cooed a woman who, according to the advert, 'knows that when it comes to choosing a refrigerator…there's enough room inside to take a banquet… Lots of refrigerated storage space means lots of advantages. You can do your week's shopping in a day…here is the refrigerator to give you a fresh interest in food, more fun and more leisure. And remember…it fits any moderate-sized kitchen comfortably!' There were 'eye-level' grills to sigh for, vacuum cleaners that made 'cleaning fun', and women were portrayed holding the flex as if they were taking a Pekinese for a walk. Spending on electrical goods and consumer durables rose six times faster than spending on other consumer items.

Washing machines – which in the early 1950s would have cost the equivalent of six weeks' average wages – were by the late-1950s standard household items, though most early models were top-loading and needed vigilance to operate them. Washing powder 'added brightness to whiteness' with Omo; or threatened that everyone would be able to tell if you were not a 'Persil' mum, since only Persil 'washes whiter' – and around £7 million was spent annually on advancing the claims of various washing powders. (Washing machines were particularly big business, since the new man-made fabrics like nylon were 'easy-care' but attracted dirt, so needed frequent washing.) There were kitchen units brand-named 'leisure' (even though not long ago 'work stations' had seemed the desirable nomenclature), and the growth of frozen foods – though most seemed to be peas, fish fingers or strawberry mousse – to pop in your new refrigerator promised more leisure, though perhaps not *The Joy of Cooking*.

In 1956 this changing pattern was reflected in new markers in the official cost-of-living (retail prices) index. Soda water, dog food, nylons, apples and pears, telephone rentals and camera films were among the items that now replaced such pre-war necessities as lump sugar, rabbits, candles and turnips.[19]

In 1958 hire-purchase restrictions were finally abolished, and by 1960 four out of five British families had hire-purchase commitments, to the tune of £1,000 million-worth of goods. A Ford Popular could be yours for a down payment of £4. 8s. 5d, while a fridge required a deposit of £3. 3s. 3d. – and in both cases the repayment period stretched into years.[20] A 1956 survey showed that half of all television sets and one-third of all vacuum cleaners were being bought on the 'never never'. 'The whole nation has taken to buying everything on the instalment plan,' Mr Isaac Wolfson, chairman of Great Universal Stores, cheerfully told his shareholders in 1958 – with only slight exaggeration. 'Who is Buying the New Consumer Goods?' queried the *Daily Herald*, and answered confidently, on the basis of 'statistical proof', that 'in the last five years or so the skilled and unskilled manual workers have emerged as the biggest spenders on a whole range of goods traditionally regarded as "middle-class products"'.[21] It was hard to believe that Ernest Bevin had not so long ago told an American audience, 'half our trouble in England is that we suffer from a poverty of desire'.[22]

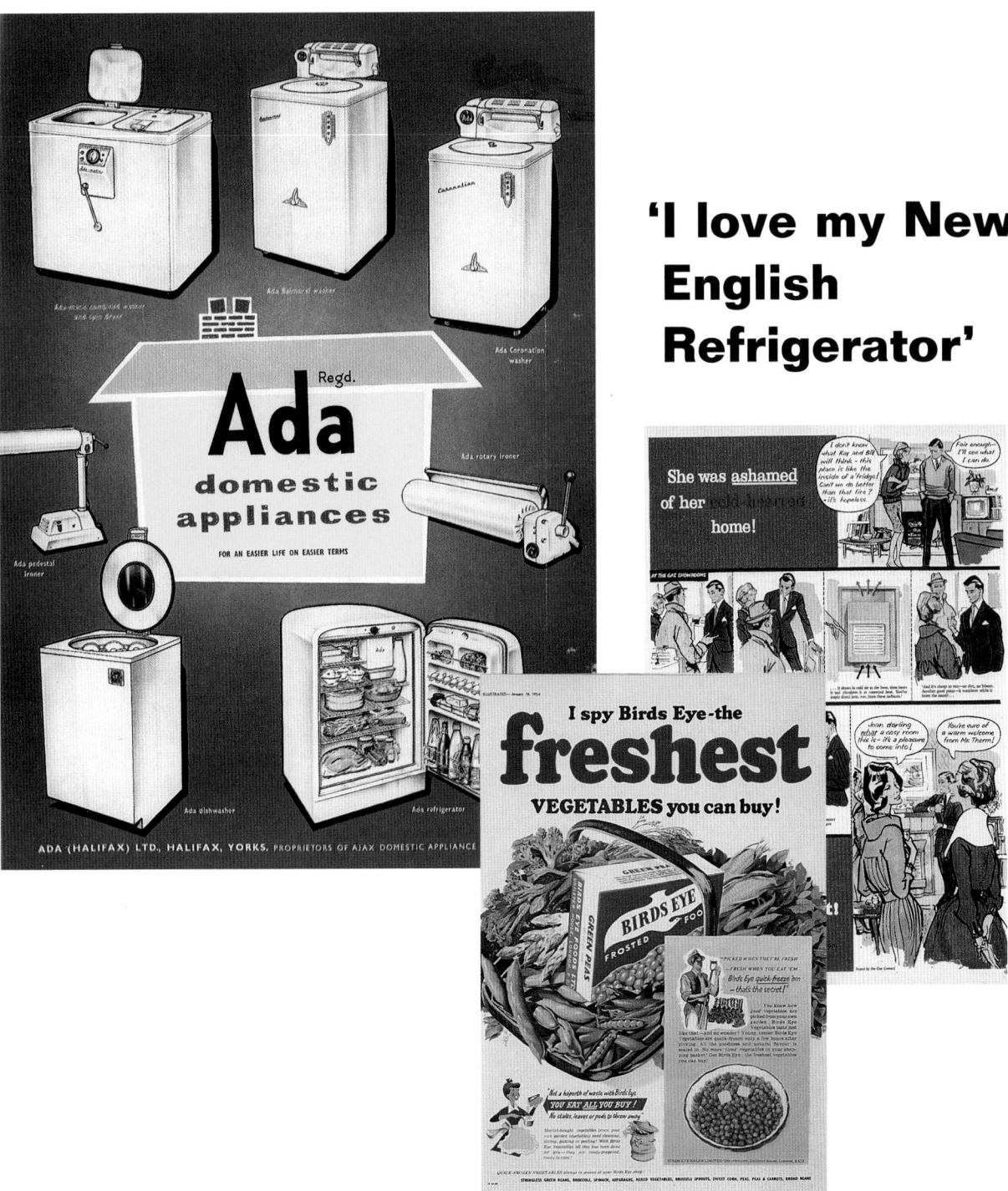

'I love my New English Refrigerator'

Above
THE POLITICS OF
SHOPPING
'Mr Cube' the sugar lump,
recruited by the
manufacturers Tate & Lyle
in their 1950 campaign
against nationalization,
and an early supermarket
photographed to support
Picture Post's assertion in
November 1955 that 'the
price to be paid for super-
efficiency, super-
cleanliness and super-
quality, is
impersonalness'.

The new home-making professional who held the domestic purse strings was not short of advice: the sale of weekly women's magazines costing 4½d. and containing adverts for 'consumer durables'; but also a plethora of domestic advice from knitting patterns, recipes and how to be well dressed on a typist's pay, to how to crochet a dressing-table set, tat a collar, make a parchment lampshade or keep your husband attentive and your children 'free from winter colds'. In 1938 *Woman* sold 75,000 copies each week; by 1952 sales had risen to 2,225,000 and by 1957 – when it was being read by one out of every two women in the country aged between sixteen and forty-four – its circulation was 3,500,000.[23] Newspapers responded to 'women's interests', and female journalists were much in evidence giving the 'women's angle' on issues; even *The Times* started a 'woman's page'. In 1957 the Consumers' Association was founded, and soon the circulation of its subscription magazine *Which?* – which could help you find the best value in appliances, from hairdriers to food mixers, and also put the claims of detergent and shampoo manufacturers through stringent scientific tests in 'laboratory conditions' – reached 300,000 copies, almost as many as *The Times*.[24]

But shopping was still a time-consuming exercise, queuing up at the baker, the butcher, the grocer and the greengrocer, and possibly the ironmonger and haberdasher too. In 1950 Sainsbury's, a long-established grocery chain, opened what was then called a 'self-service' shop in Croydon and the following year Earls Court boasted a 'supermarket'. The era of the wire basket, and later the shopping trolley, had dawned.

'Togetherness' was part of the nesting dream and nowhere was coupledom sold with such tenacity as in the 'do-it-yourself' market. Home-owners had the incentive to decorate and 'improve' their homes and, now with shorter working hours, weekends – at least after Saturday lunchtime – free and paid holidays, the time to do it. But again, do-it-yourself had to be distanced from the dreariness of wartime make-overs. It had to be fun. In the mid-1950s, the magazine *Woman* renamed its 'Make Do and Mend' advice column 'Tackle it Together', and in 1957 two new DIY magazines appeared: *Practical Householder* and *Do it Yourself.* Though these were targeted at 'the practical man about the house', tending to regard 'soft furnishings' as the woman's department, while it was the man who wielded the drill and chisel, the ethos was betrayed by the 'miracle' products over which it eulogized, since it was obvious that two pairs of hands were needed to stick on wipe-down Formica tops, self-assemble furniture or even screw in hand-crafted plywood curtain pelmets and pegboards. Almost three-quarters of the wallpaper sold by the end of the 1950s was over the counter to householders rather than professional decorators; the sale of electric drills soared; and the words 'all you need is a screwdriver' seemed a welcome challenge to many, as self-assembly furniture started appearing in the shops.

'Togetherness' in a family, home-based sense was reinforced by another 1950s' development: television. Television had been in its infancy when the war had caused its shut-down in the middle of a Mickey Mouse cartoon on 1 September 1939. It resumed on 7 June 1946, picking up where Mickey had been left seven years before. However, by 1950 only 350,000 households possessed a walnut-veneered set with double doors closed over the nine- or ten-inch screen in the corner of their living room, and two years later only two million sets had been sold.

The turning point came with the Coronation of Elizabeth II in June 1953. Her father, George VI, had died in his sleep

Left
HOME-MADE FASHION
In the 1950s, dressmaking patterns, like these from a 1951 issue of *My Home*, recipes, beauty hints and romantic fiction were the staple fare of most women's magazines.

Below
VICTOR SYLVESTER'S BALLROOM DANCING CLUB (1955)
This programme started on BBC television in 1948 and featured live bands playing music to a strict tempo, essential for all ballroom twirlings.

THE TIMES
EVEREST
COLOUR SUPPLEMENT
LONDON   1953   PRICE 3s. 6d.

COMPANIONS IN ACHIEVEMENT
Sir Edmund Hillary and Tensing Norkey, G.M., who together climbed Everest on Friday, May 29, 1953.

on 6 February 1952 and the 24-year-old Princess had been recalled from Kenya where she was on a tour her father had been too ill to undertake, to take the throne. The Coronation was planned as a major national event – the Elizabethan age was to dawn with pomp and ceremony, in affirmation of a monarchy that had grown popular through the steadfastness of the King and Queen in sharing in the people's war. The coronation robes were to be designed by Norman Hartnell, who had also designed the Princess's dress when she was married in November 1947. But this time there was not the same post-war miasma of restrictions, which had meant that although the wedding dress was 'embroidered and decorated on a scale well beyond the reach of any but royalty', the couturier had been allowed only a hundred clothing coupons and 'this had had to cover a bridal train that stretched fourteen yards behind her'. Then Hartnell had had 'to ensure

that the future Queen of England was not wearing anything that came from ex-enemy territory', so 'the 10,000 tiny seed pearls with which the dress was oversewn were ordered from the United States', and a Scottish firm based near Dunfermline and Hartnell's staff were obliged to 'hunt round for silkworms that came neither from Italy, nor from Japan.'[25]

But in 1953, the royal dressmaker had a free rein and his 'second masterpiece' was 'adorned with the symbols of England, Scotland, Ireland and Wales…the rose, the thistle, the shamrock and the leek – each emblem appearing on the skirt in strict order of precedence'. Meanwhile 'the lower half of the robe was embellished with the combined flowers of the Commonwealth countries…nestling round the motherly Tudor rose of England'.[26] The new Queen was to drive to Westminster Abbey in a golden coach of Cinderella magnificence, followed by her consort, Prince Philip, and her

Facing page
THE ASCENT OF EVEREST
The news that 'Everest has been conquered at last' reached Britain on the eve of the Coronation. In a party planned and led by Colonel John Hunt, the New Zealander Edmund Hillary and Tensing Norkey (known as Sherpa Tensing to the British) planted a Union Jack, Stars and Stripes and UN flag on the pinnacle. *The Times* produced a commemorative supplement.

Above
CORONATION LONDON
London's Oxford Street decorated for the Coronation of Elizabeth II. The procession passed along this main thoroughfare.

Right
THE ROYAL FAMILY
The cover of *John Bull* with a painting of the Queen dressed for Trooping the Colour in June 1953, a week after the Coronation, with Prince Charles and Princess Anne.

Below
THE CORONATION PROCESSION
The Queen in the Golden Coach pulled by six grey horses turning out of the Mall towards Buckingham Palace on the return from Westminster Abbey on 2 June 1953.

visitors and subjects from all over the world, who were to prove a great attraction to the watching crowds, particularly the gracious and friendly Queen Salote of Tonga. They were watched by some 30,000 people who had slept in the Mall, newspapers wrapped round their legs to keep out the rain and cold, in order to be in at the start of the new Elizabethan Age.

Not surprisingly, the BBC had decided that the ceremony in the Abbey should be televised. The request was rejected by the Duke of Norfolk, the Earl Marshal of England who was orchestrating the event, and by the Archbishop of Canterbury, neither of whom could see how such a solemn moment could retain its dignity if it was beset with cables, booms and camera men. It took months of persuasion before the Establishment relented and the authoritative and portly figure of radio commentator Richard Dimbleby was allowed to climb into his soundproof box high above the nave before dawn on 2 June, with his carefully prepared index cards, to give the more than twenty million viewers at home two and a half hours of viewing; this included close-ups of the Queen's face, and a far better view of the proceedings than any of the actual guests in the Abbey had.

After that television became something to save for or, more likely, buy on HP (hire purchase), and by 1959 a survey revealed that 60 per cent of British adults were tuned in every evening for a period of five hours in the winter and three and a half in the summer.[27] But in the early 1950s there was no question of being a total couch-potato. Viewing hours were limited, with transmission from 3 p.m. on weekdays and 5 p.m. on Sundays and close-down at 10.30 p.m., except at times of great moment when the screen might be allowed to flicker on for an extra quarter of an hour. There was also a 'toddler's truce' between 6 and 7 p.m. to ensure that children were put to bed at a proper hour.[28] Even then, transmission

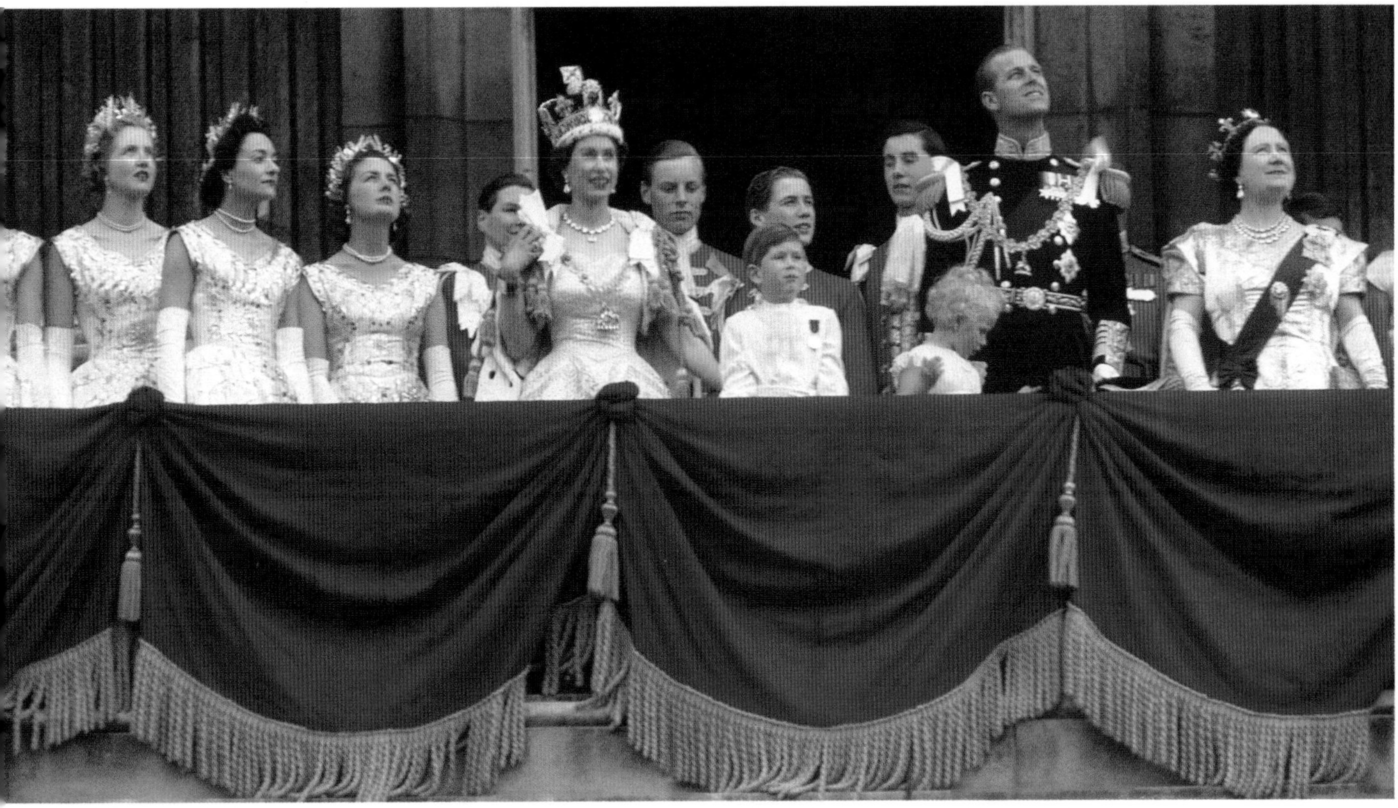

was not continuous: 'interludes', like computer screen-savers of windmills, waves breaking or a potter's wheel turning, punctuated the evening.[29]

The programmes were largely of an instructional type: cookery hints from Philip Harben, the goatee-bearded chef in a blue-and-white striped butcher's apron; or gardening tips from 'Mr Middleton', until he died and was succeeded in the cabbage patch by Fred Streeter. And for children's entertainment there were puppet shows: Muffin the Mule with Annette Mills, when children were instructed to sing 'We love Muffin, Muffin the Mule' every time the jerky marionette hove into view; Mr Turnip Head; the strangulated and repetitious ramblings of Bill and Ben the Flowerpot Men with their companion 'Little Weed'; and Andy Pandy, whose simple, slow pleasures carry some genetic link to today's Teletubbies. By 1955 the BBC reported that 85 per cent of

Above
HAPPY AND GLORIOUS
The newly-crowned Queen Elizabeth II with Prince Philip, the Queen Mother, Prince Charles and Princess Anne on the balcony of Buckingham Palace, watch an RAF fly past tribute.

Left
STREET CELEBRATIONS
A Coronation street party in the East End of London, with presents for the children.

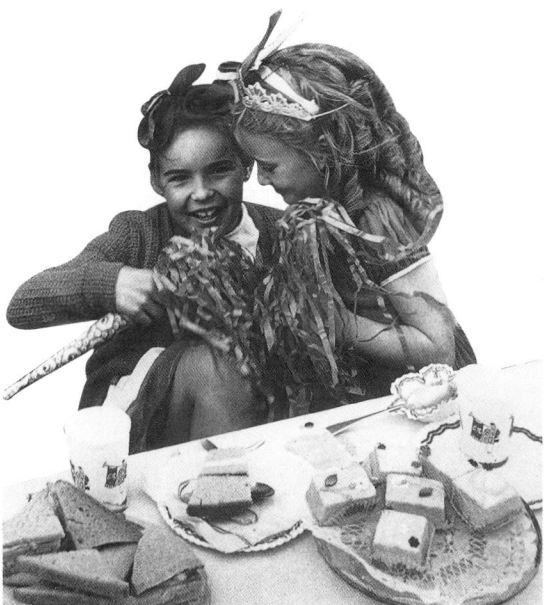

june whitfield

The actress June Whitfield shot to national fame with her radio appearance in 1953 as Eth, the long-suffering fiancée of Ron Glum (Dick Bentley).

'Originally the Glums were a five-minute episode in the Frank Muir and Denis Norden series *Take It From Here* which had first been broadcast in 1948. But soon the Glums, who Muir and Norden had introduced to the rather cosy other offerings of the period, proved so popular that the serial was expanded to fill half the show's thirty-minutes.

The programme, with Jimmy Edwards as Pa Glum (the forerunner to Alf Garnett), attracted an audience of 22 million at its peak: it was recorded in front of a live audience and went out at lunch time on Sundays and again on a weekday evening – so there was no excuse not to gather round the bakelite set to catch every episode.

It reflected the mores of the period – Ron and Eth remained engaged – 'on the brink', with Pa Glum's interruptions meaning that their interminable courtship 'was like driving a car with one foot on the brake and the other on the accelerator'. Then one day, Ron fell down a manhole, and that was that.'

Facing page
'OH, RON!' 'YES ETH?'
June Whitfield who
replaced Joy Nicholls as
Ron Glum's (Dick
Bentley's) fiancée, Eth, in
Take It From Here the
popular radio show in
November 1953.

Left
ON AIR
The Take It From Here
team in November 1953
(left to right) Dick
Bentley, June Whitfield,
Jimmy Edwards and Alma
Cogan, who joined the
show that month to
provide some vocals.

the home-grown *Sunday Night at the London Palladium* and *Robin Hood*, and quiz shows that mimicked the American *$64 Question* in all but the largesse of their prizes. Be the fortunate winner on Hughie Green's *Double Your Money* or Michael Miles' *Take Your Pick* and you could walk away with £100 or a refrigerator.

Commercial television had predictably been opposed as being trivial by the Reithian BBC and by what came to be seen as the 'Establishment' generally, who believed in a patrician form of public-service broadcasting, and that the public could not always be trusted not to go for the lowest common denominator – look at America! The programmes on British commercial television were not sponsored by advertisers on this model, but by a series of regional companies that were franchised to provide programmes and to sell advertising – and, in the words of Roy Thomson, the Canadian founder of Scottish television and, on the back of its success, owner of *The Sunday Times*, 'a licence to print money'. And although ITV fulfilled the Cassandras' prophecies with its game shows and endless American imports of cowboys and domestic comedies, it also pioneered news programmes like *Tonight* (which finally put the kibosh on 'Toddler's Truce') and *Panorama*, fronted by Richard Dimbleby. These attracted a weekly audience of eight or nine million, and were 'in-depth' programmes that questioned as well as reported and were, in many ways, the animated equivalent of the magazine *Picture Post*'s searching and sometimes uncomfortable journalism. Indeed it was with the arrival of these programmes, as well as a new breed of 'newscasters' like Robin Day and Ludovic Kennedy (who were journalists rather than bulletin readers), that *Picture Post*, by now something of a shadow of its earlier critical self – ceased publication in 1957. It had been discredited in

five- to seven-year-olds watched television daily, and dentists issued warnings about a nation of buck-toothed adults, if children persisted in watching 'the box' lying on the floor with their chin cupped in their hands.[30]

Once the children were in bed there were panel games like *What's My Line?*, in which well-bred, elegantly dressed and coiffeured panellists like Katie Boyle, Isabel Barnett, plus the irascible Gilbert Harding, tried to guess what unusual or frankly risible trade a contestant pursued. Peter Lewis explains in his book on the 1950s that many entertainers' agents were opposed to their clients appearing on television, believing that a lifetime's material would be used up in a single evening of mass viewing.[31] It was not until the launch of commercial – or, as it came to be called, 'independent' – television on 22 September 1955 that entertainment took on a more popular coloration, with US imports like *I Love Lucy*,

many people's eyes by the refusal of its owner, Edward Hulton, to publish James Cameron's story and Bert Hardy's photographs of the barbarous treatment of North Korean refugees by the British- and American-supported south.

In the early days of television, visual media had seemed to be a supplement to audio: just four pages at the back of the *Radio Times* were devoted to television, and 'wireless' programmes still drew regular audiences in their hundreds of thousands, for whom radio was no white noise but part of the family schedule of gathering round the wireles to listen to the 1950s successors to the wartime successes such as ITMA (*It's That Man Again*) with Tommy Handley. There was *Take it From Here*, written by Frank Muir and Dennis Norden, with Jimmy Edwards as the father of the gormless Ron (Dick Bentley) and his long-suffering fiancée, Eth (June Whitfield); *Educating Archie*, in which Peter Brough talked to his ventriloquist's dummy, and then answered himself, though since it was radio no one could see who was talking anyway; the harsh sounds of Billy Cotton's *Wakey, Waaakey* opening his *Band Show*; the slightly surrealistic and certainly *risqué Much Binding in the Marsh*, with Richard Murdoch and a camp Kenneth Williams; there were the *Adventures of Dick Barton*, *Jennings and Darbyshire* for children, and *Toytown* with L-L-Larry the Lamb and Mr Growser, the 'German sausage-dog' (dachshund), for younger children.

There were the serials: the twice-daily *Mrs Dale's Diary*, in which Mrs Dale (played by Ellis Powell)'s anxious 'I'm worried about Jim' became a national catchphrase; its rural –

Above
'50s TELEVISION FOR TEENAGERS
Six Five Special: the presenters were Pete (later Peter) Murray and Jo Douglas. It showcased such stars as skiffle-king Lonnie Donegan and, on this occasion, Joyce Shock, the 20-year-old former secretary of the crooner, Frankie Vaughan, making her television debut singing in November 1957.

Right
MY FAIR LADY
Programme for *My Fair Lady* a musical adaptation of George Bernard Shaw's novel *Pygmalion* which opened in London on 30 April 1958 with lavish sets designed by Cecil Beaton. Shaw can be seen as an angel manipulating Rex Harrison as Professor Henry Higgins, who in turn is pulling the strings of the flowerseller, Eliza Doolittle, played by Julie Andrews.

Far right
THE GOONS
An ensemble of Bluebottle, Eccles, Minnie Bannister, Major Bloodknock and company aka the Goons (left to right) Peter Sellers, Harry Secombe, Spike Milligan and Michael Bentine recording an episode in May 1951 when the programme was called *Crazy People*. The name was changed to The *Goon Show* in 1952.

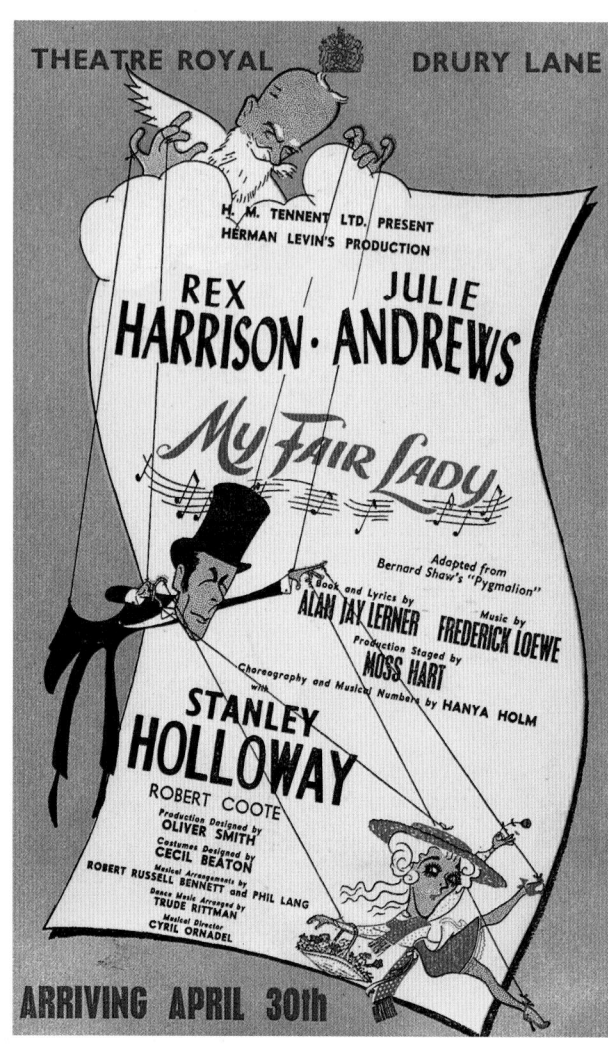

and information-packed – counterpart *The Archers* (1951), which achieved notoriety when a key character, Grace Archer, perished in a fire at her stables the night that ITV was launched; and a series of adventures for grown-ups such as *Paul Temple*, in which the heroine and Paul's fellow-detective, Steve, was imagined to be willowy and blonde 'because of her voice'. There was *Two Way Family Favourites*, records requested by and for servicemen and -women and for men doing their National Service; and there was Wilfred Pickles with his peripatetic, meet-the-people slot, *Have a Go*, with Mabel (Mrs Pickles) 'at the table' to reward any local colour who gamely obeyed the call.

There was also serious and experimental drama: Harold Pinter's and John Mortimer's work was first heard on the radio: Samuel Beckett's next pronouncement after *Waiting for Godot* was a broadcast play; and in 1953 a verse drama by the recently – and prematurely – deceased Welsh poet Dylan Thomas, *Under Milk Wood*, was first broadcast: 'It is spring, moonless night in the small town, starless and bibleblack…sloeblack, slow, black, crowblack, fishingboat-bobbing sea…' sounded the sonorous tones of the narrator Richard Burton, telling of the doings of Llaregyb (rather than Llareggub, as Thomas called it, because spelled backwards it characterized what happened in his home village of Laugharne, on which the play was based).

And there were two comedy shows that are now classics and which in the 1950s had a cult following such that their phrases entered the nation's lexicon, so that you only had to say 'Bluebottle' or 'Eccles' in a particular quavering way to have everyone in the office, on the factory floor or in the Junior Common Room cracking up. *Hancock's Half Hour*, written by Ray Galton and Alan Simpson, which chronicled the life of the gloomy, self-improving social commentator

Anthony Aloysius Hancock at Railway Cuttings, East Cheam – where he verbally sparred with and tried to educate a cockney wide-boy and 'poltroon', Sid James, and a solicitous, conciliatory Hattie Jacques – was first heard on air in 1954 and transferred to television in 1956. But one show that could never make a successful transition to the visual was the surrealistic, anarchic *Goon Show*, which was first heard on radio in 1951. Largely scripted by Spike Milligan and starring him, Harry Secombe, Peter Sellers (and in the beginning Michael Bentine), it was a department of funny voices and long-drawn-out sound effects of such previously unheard events as exploding shirt-tails and walking backwards to Christmas. It challenged authority with its infantile voices, literal logic and its lunatic characters like Major Bloodknock, which spoke to a generation who had endured too many rules, regulations and petty bullying in

Above
STAR VEHICLE
All the stars of the silver screen were found in the weekly fan magazine *Picturegoer*. This issue is from October 1957 when in fact the cinema was losing out to television. Kay Kendall, the British actress, fronts the galaxy of big names inside.

the barrack rooms of war and National Service. But it did not please the BBC, and in 1959 the Goons gave up.

Television brought the world to your sitting room – and for many it dampened the enthusiasm for going out to see in the flesh what you could happily watch, perched on a leatherette pouf or G-plan sofa, with a 'TV dinner' in a sectioned tinfoil tray, accompanied by a bottle of beer (draught beer sales had been falling since the advent of television) in the comfort of your own home. Attendance at football matches, which had peaked in the immediate post-war years, declined as armchair watching lessened the attraction of stadium stands, and other sports suffered a similar decline. Cinema attendance, which had occupied on average one night every week for one-third of the entire British population in 1946,[32] equally declined with the advent of television.

Hollywood hit back with a big-screen strategy of Cinemascope and other 'special-effect' biblical epics: *Quo Vadis* (1951, the highest grosser for MGM after *Gone With the Wind* and featuring what seemed like half of Italy as Roman troops); *The Robe* (1953); *The Ten Commandments* (1956); the four-hour *Ben-Hur* (1959); and it made Technicolor films of the musicals that had so brightened and lightened the London stage in the immediate post-war years: *Annie Get Your Gun, Oklahoma!, Singin' in the Rain, The King and I*. The British film industry continued the success it had achieved with the brilliant Ealing comedies of the late 1940s by redeploying their stars – Alec Guinness, Alistair Sim and Margaret Rutherford – in more films about British eccentrics or, in the case of Alec Guinness, a confrontation with one of the worst British war experiences in *The Bridge on the River Kwai* (1957). But by the end of the decade, this nostalgia for

British ways and heroics had begun to seem whimsical, and a harder, grittier realism arrived in the cinema.

But if TV made the British people armchair spectators of a world in which they had once been more active participants, then the late 1950s saw a connection with that wider world and a broadening of horizons and of expectations. In Len Deighton's novel *The Ipcress File*, published in 1962, the hero recounts, 'I walked down Charlotte Street towards Soho… I bought two packets of Gauloises, sank a quick grappa with Mario and Franco at the Terrazzo, bought a *Statesman*, some Normandy butter and garlic sausage…'[33] The 'Continent' was now chic – and part of British life, with pizza being advertised in a Leicester Square restaurant as 'Italian Welsh rarebit'.

In 1951, 'when food rationing was still in force', Elizabeth David's *French Country Cooking* was published, in which she described French meals using 'quantities of bacon, cream, eggs, meat stock' and then gave the recipes for these gustatory dreams with suggestions of 'what ingredients might be substituted from the Englishwoman's store cupboard' and a section of 'recipes dealing with tinned food'. In 1959 the book was revised and published as a Penguin paperback, with the substitutes withdrawn, the tinned food notions banished. While Elizabeth David did not overnight transform the British table from one serving quantities of mince and overcooked, watery vegetables, with plums and custard for afters and powdered coffee – or liquid Camp – she was part of a revolution that slowly brought style and pleasure to a country that had been light on such commodities for more than a decade. 'It is another world from ours,' eulogized the *Sunday Times*' reviewer, 'it knows nothing of the ready-packaged product, the five-second whip-up; here food is treated with reverence.' But David was prescribing more than

Above
COFFEE BAR CULTURE
The Italianization of London style introduced gleaming, hissing espresso-machine cafés which proved groovy haunts for the young. This one was in Kensington High Street (1955): the most famous was the '2 i s' in Old Compton Street, Soho where Tommy Steele started his singing career.

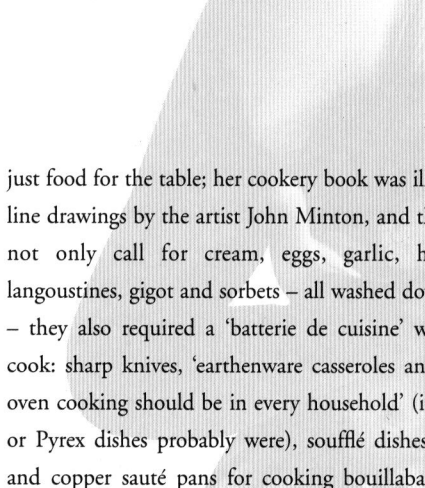

**Right
ALMA COGAN,**
The girl 'with the chuckle
in her voice' and an
extensive stage wardrobe
of flouncey, sparkly
dresses which she
designed herself, was one
of Britain's most popular
recording stars in the
'50s. Her string of hits
included 'Dreamboat' the
only record by a female
British singer to reach
number one in the 1950s.

just food for the table; her cookery book was illustrated with line drawings by the artist John Minton, and the recipes did not only call for cream, eggs, garlic, herbs, olives, langoustines, gigot and sorbets – all washed down with wine – they also required a 'batterie de cuisine' with which to cook: sharp knives, 'earthenware casseroles and terrines for oven cooking should be in every household' (in fact enamel or Pyrex dishes probably were), soufflé dishes, bain-maries and copper sauté pans for cooking bouillabaisse. It was a quality of life, now that there was more money and more leisure, and more value being put on what was beginning to be called 'lifestyle'.

For the young it meant the Italianization of style – the new phenomenon of espresso coffee bars (only the British made them more 'of the moment' by pronouncing it 'expresso'), which served 'froffy coffee' and where they could sit for hours talking after they had been thrown out of the listening booths of record shops for requesting to hear the latest single from Frankie Vaughan or Alma Cogan, but not buying. Books to be seen reading came from France and Italy too – Jean-Paul Sartre's *Nausea*; *Bonjour Tristesse*, a worldly, cynical little book by nineteen-year-old Parisian, Françoise Sagan; or, in a rather different vein, Alberto Moravio's explicit *Woman of Rome*.

Gina Lollobrigida smouldered and Brigette Bardot pouted and frolicked on the cinema screen, and influenced young women who probably never actually got to see *And God Created Woman* into wearing stiletto heels, sheer nylons (at last), low-cut, cleavage-revealing broderie anglaise tops, or tight sweaters, clinched at the waist with a wide plastic belt or cummerbund; they popularized full flouncy skirts (of pink gingham, if it was Bardot who was your inspiration) that

stuck out at an almost horizontal angle, made by dipping petticoats in a sugar-and-water solution, or by threading them with plastic hoops like a (shrunken) Victorian crinoline. And to complete the cosmopolitan look, in a nation of women who had not long before found it essential to cram a felt or straw hat on their head and gloves on their hands before venturing into a public place – a headscarf; no longer flapping in a triangle as shoppers had worn them in the queuing days of austerity, but tied (balaclava-like) in a fashion that owed much to that perfect cool, elegant English rose, the American screen actress, Grace Kelly who, before the decade was out, was actually to marry a prince.

By the end of the 1950s the films that made the news all came from the Continent – Fellini's satyric masterpieces and the beginning of *la nouvelle vague*, with François Truffaut's *Les Quatre Cent Coups* (1959); Alain Resnais' addictively mysterious *Last Year at Marienbad* (1961) and the haunting *Hiroshima mon amour* (1959), which confirmed that the atom bomb had done even more than wipe out two cities; it had suffused the sentience of the century.

The smartest way for the young to travel was no longer by bike or even motorcycle; it was on a rather feminized, zippy little Italian-made Lambretta or Vespa scooter. For families, cars were getting more affordable, and although there were still plenty of motor-cycles with side-cars going on expeditions, a car was what most families aspired to. In 1948 there were just over two million private cars on British roads; in 1938 there had been just under that figure. It was not until 1955 that the figure rose to over three and a half million.[34] Roads were still poor, with dual carriageways the exception, and a family travelling from the home counties to the West Country for a holiday might leave home almost before dawn,

B.O.A.C

B.O.A.C., which was formed in November 1939 from the merger of Imperial Airways and British Airways, girdled the globe ever faster: in October 1958 the Corporation introduced the first scheduled transatlantic jet service.

with sandwiches and a thermos packed, in the hope of making Torquay or Truro by winding trunk roads, with legendary queues on the Honiton bypass, in time for a wash before tea. An Austin A40 cost £685, and there was no speed limit on out of town roads, no breathalyzer, no seat belts. But domination of the car was relentless: London trams were retired in 1952; the last steam locomotive was built in 1958; and in 1963 Dr Beeching's axe fell on branch railway lines, reducing the network from 13,000 to 8,000 miles.

Meanwhile, by 1965 there were over nine million cars on British roads; parking meters had been introduced in 1958 to try to limit the number of cars clogging city streets; the next year Sir Christopher Cockerell's Hovercraft, designed to carry cars across the Channel on a cushion of air, came into service; and in 1958 the first British motorway, the Preston bypass was opened; in 1959 Ernie Marples, Minister of Transport, proudly cut the tape on the first stretch of the M1. The motorway's blue traffic signs remain. In those first years cars from the British Cadillac equivalent – the Ford Zephyr to the slipstream pod, the Jaguar E type (first made in 1961) – roared up the fast lane, until in 1964 a 70 m.p.h. speed limit was introduced.

And if you could not visit friends and family, you could now telephone them. By 1951 only 1.5 million households had a private telephone: most people had to pop to the red telephone box, feed in pennies, ponder which end of the receiver you spoke into and press 'button A' when connected. By 1966 that figure had increased fourfold, but by the end of the 1960s more than half the homes in Britain were still without a private phone. STD (subscriber trunk dialling), which bypassed calling the operator for every number, was first introduced in Bristol in 1958 and came to London by 1960, gradually spreading throughout the whole country.[35]

It was not just Britain that was getting smaller, so was the world: the first direct table link transatlantic telephone service came into operation in 1956; BOAC's Comet was the first jet airline to fly the Atlantic on scheduled flights, and this signalled the not-so-slow demise of ocean liners as a means of travelling directly. A continental holiday now became a reality. Tourist fares had first been introduced on airlines in 1952 and soon mushrooming travel agencies were reducing the cost of holidays abroad by chartering planes to take people on 'package tours' to Spain, Italy, Switzerland or Austria. Meanwhile those who wanted to see more than a beach, were off on confusing, 'if it's Wednesday it must be Heidelberg' continental, air-conditioned coach trips. National Service had opened the eyes of many to 'abroad' and by 1958 the number of Britons travelling there (invariably to Europe) for their holidays reached two million, almost twice what it had been at its highest point before the war; the Automobile Association, which helped motorists arrange these things, reported that two-thirds of their members had taken their cars abroad during the 1950s.[36] 'Hitch hiking' was beginning to be a means by which the young (those who were not young gentlemen sent on an educative 'Grand Tour') got to see the wonders of the world (still European) beyond their own shores, and even that replica of Britain at play, Butlins, opened foreign travel agencies. 'It is quite possible,' *The Times* reported in 1956, 'that the porter who carries your cases at Waterloo or Victoria has just returned from San Sebastián, or the South of France.'

On 15 November 1957, Macmillan repeated the words 'they've never had it so good' that he had said earlier in the year, but he went on to reflect: 'The luxuries of the rich have become the necessities of the poor, but people are asking "what is it all for?"' [37]

jocelyn stevens

Above
SOCIETY WEDDING
Jocelyn Stevens, marries
Jane Sheffield in June
1956 – a year before he
bought *Queen*.

Above right
FASHION CAN BE FUN
The cover of *The Queen*
for September 1960, the
year designated by the
magazine as a 'Year for
Swindles'. 'The greatest
illusion is that 'we've
never had it so good' yet
'over 1 million people are
living below the
subsistence level'.

Facing page
MAC THE MAN
May 1963 issue which
ran an interview on
Macmillan by Jocelyn
Stevens.

'I bought *The Queen* on February 14th 1957... That August I ran a story on the 'beautiful people of Venice'...I called Peggy Guggenheim "The Most Dotty"... She issued a writ. Against my lawyer's advice I wrote her a long letter in which I set out to establish that all the great men and women in history were 'dotty'. She wrote back saying it was the most dotty letter she had ever received and forgave me...

I still believe that Henri Cartier-Bresson is the greatest features photographer of all time...in 1959 we were able to secure the British rights of the astonishing coverage of Red China he had just completed... We published 80 pages of Red China, spread over four issues. Many readers wrote in saying they didn't buy *The Queen* to read about Red China. I had a slip printed stating that the Editor-in-Chief was more interested in what was going on in China than in what was going on in Society at present, and if they did not share his views they were advised not to buy the magazine again. It was about this time that we began to question the accepted obsequious coverage of Society and its attitudes that had emerged unscathed from the pre-war years.'[38]

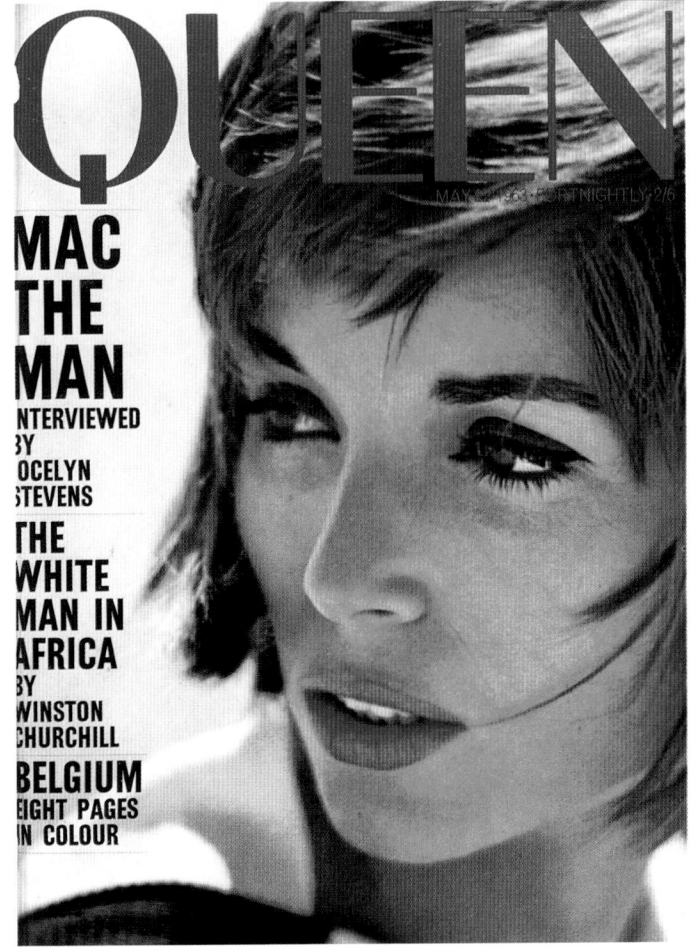

LIVE IT UP!

PART 1

LONDON
RECORDS

RE-F 1049

LIVE IT UP
REAL ROCK DRIVE
TEN LITTLE INDIANS
CHATTANOOGA CHOO CHOO

BILL
HALEY
AND HIS COMETS

45 R.P.M. EXTENDED PLAY RECORD

youthquake

Above
FUTURISTIC FASHION
In 1965 *The Observer*
colour supplement called
the fashions of designer
Courrèges 'clothes of the
future'. They were
infinitely photographable
for the glossy magazines
and new Sunday
newspaper supplements
that sold unobtainable
style perfection and acres
of advertising space.

'England exploded, didn't it?' reminisced Paul McCartney in December 1965. 'I don't know when…' There were many claims for the date of the explosion, the seismic shift along the generational fault-line that reverberated through politics, the economy, social attitudes, education, consumer spending, sexual mores, music, art, the theatre, literature, design, fashion – and, above all, expectations.

At the start of the decade, on 3 February 1960, the Prime Minister Harold Macmillan spoke of the 'Winds of Change' that were beginning to blow. He was speaking of Africa – and sooner than he could have imagined the winds there turned to a tornado, when within weeks the massacre at Sharpeville and the subsequent assassination attempt on the life of the President, Dr Voerwood, brought the nature of black oppression and apartheid sharply into focus for the British. But although it did not seem so at the time, those winds were not confined to the veldt. At the 1959 election, the Tory slogan had been 'Life is Better Under the Conservatives. Don't Let Labour Ruin It'. It was a hard proposition to dispute in economic terms. In that spring's budget the standard rate of income tax had been cut from 8s. 6d. in the pound to 7s. 9d., a rate not matched until Thatcher's premiership in the 1980s, despite a sterling crisis less than two years before that suggested that government spending was out of control. Even the *Daily Mirror* started to publish a City page, so that its thirteen million largely working-class readers could watch their stocks and shares[1] – or at least feel part of the ever onwards and upwards financial boom.

Despite the Liberal leader Jo Grimond electioneering by helicopter in a thoroughly modern manner in the 1959 General Election and urging Britain 'to get into Europe' without delay – while Labour ran a broadly united and credible campaign suggesting that it really was an alternate government, with a bright young politician, Anthony Wedgwood Benn, competently orchestrating the new political medium of television to get a centrist message across to the electorate – the pendulum failed to swing. The Conservatives increased their majority for the fourth time: the party led by a relation (by marriage) of the Duke of Devonshire, with a Cabinet one-third of whom were old Etonians, seemed invincible; and 'Supermac', the cartoonist Vicky's Macmillan character, seemed to be just that. The Labour Party wondered about a change of name, and published a pamphlet angsting 'Must Labour Lose?'; had affluence and a bi-partisan welfare state effectively eroded its constituency?

But any complacency, or 'smugness', that the *Economist* detected 'at the gates of a new decade'[2] was misplaced. Writing his memoirs, the former Conservative Lord Chancellor, Viscount Kilmuir, reflected, 'we utterly failed in these years to find a popular non-materialistic policy for the party… "You never had it so good" was true and appropriate in the context of 1959, but…lost its impact. This new feeling was difficult to define. It was "anti-Establishment" but not anarchic; it embraced no existing political philosophy; it could not be explained in class or economic terms…we were absolutely baffled by it. The return of idealism to politics caught both parties off balance, and the Conservatives suffered worst.'[3]

In August 1959, that gilded year (even the summer was exceptional, with sun and blue skies day after day) *Queen* published an article purporting to be 'The Establishment Chronicle' (based loosely on the *Eton Chronicle*), the coat of arms of which bore the vernacular legend 'Qualify, Compromise, Arrange'.[4] The magazine (which had been bought by Jocelyn Stevens on his twenty-fifth birthday in 1957) was edited by the ex-*Vogue* star, Beatrix Miller, with a

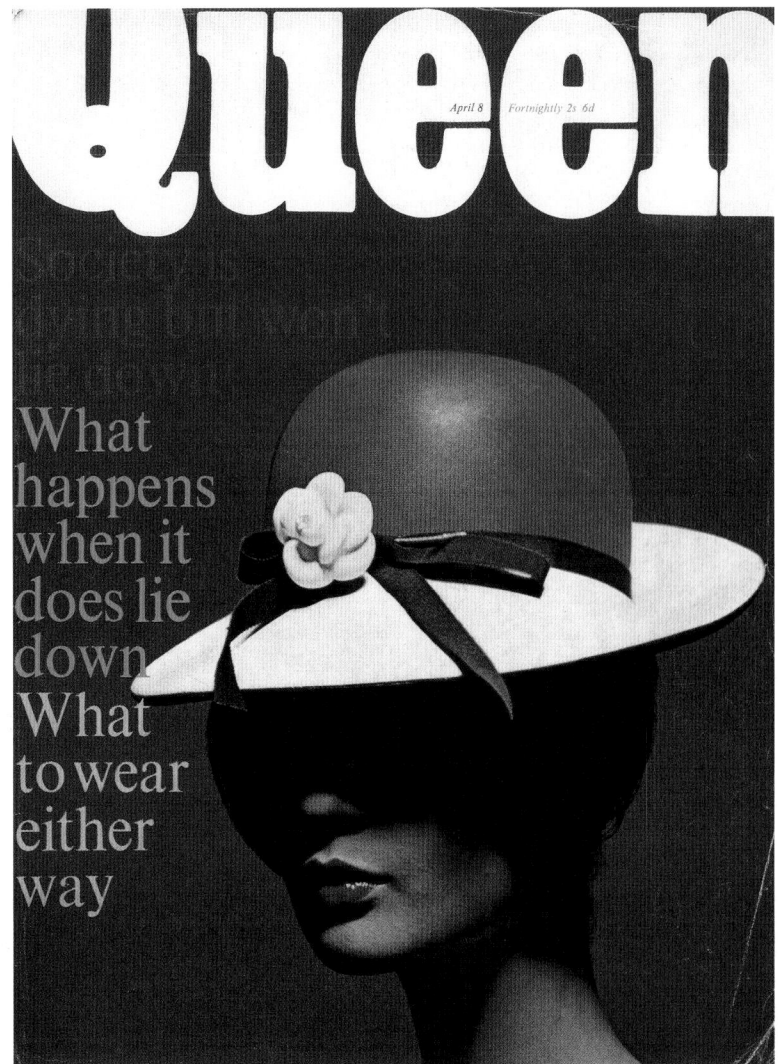

Above
HIGH SOCIETY
Queen, the society magazine that liked to ironize about its constituency. Even the adverts played the game, talking about make-up 'for a post atomic age' and claiming that a bar of plain chocolate had 'a bittersweet, Modigliani flavour' and was 'a slim, Mondrian shape' in a Rembrandt colour.

Above
PRIVATE EYE
Private Eye's 1963 take
on the Establishment: two
upper-class City types
demanding we 'get rid of
this class nonsense...'
whilst of course 'the great
strength of the British
way of life is that we don't
have revolutions'. And
Private Eye's comment
(right) on the decision of
the relatively unknown
14th Earl of Home who,
as a compromise
candidate between the
competing claims of Lord
Hailsham and R.A.Butler
on the resignation of
Macmillan, disclaimed his
title in 1963 in order to
take the leadership of the
Conservative Party, and
thus become Prime
Minister.

team of Stevens' contemporaries, including Mark Boxer as art editor, Francis Wyndham writing on the theatre, and a hot new photographer, Anthony Armstrong-Jones, taking most of the pictures. The *Queen* team also included Betty Kenward, poached from *The Tatler* to contribute a 'Jennifer's Diary' society column, in the first of which she trilled, 'the London Season has opened…I am very thrilled to have joined the enthusiastic young team (all much younger than I am!) who run this magazine with such verve'.[5]

The rules of the 'Establishment', according to *Queen*, magazine stated:

1. The aim of the Establishment is to run the country.
2. Membership is restricted to those either in a position of direct power or able to wield great personal influence.

3. No one must be allowed to achieve a position of real importance unless he is a member.

The 'Chronicle' showed an Eton school photograph with its own 'members' heads superimposed. They included Lord Mountbatten, Evelyn Waugh, Harold Macmillan, the Duke of Devonshire, Maurice Bowra, the Archbishop of Canterbury, Lord Astor, Kenneth Clark, Harold Nicolson and Isaiah Berlin, though it regretted that 'we have lost touch with the following old boys: G[uy] Burgess, D[onald] Maclean, A[nthony] Eden and O[swald] Mosley'. *The Establishment Chronicle and Nepotist's Gazette* was purportedly edited by William Haley (who was in fact editor of *The Times*, which advertised 'Top People Read *The Times*', though Haley himself had become a 'top person', rather than having been born one, since he had left school at sixteen and worked as a telephonist on the switchboard of *The Times* that he was later to edit, before becoming Director General of the BBC).[6]

At the end of the same year, *Queen* drove the point home with the headline 'A Bad Year for Dodos'[7] since, the magazine pronounced, the new decade was going to slough off the 'old firm' in politics, music, design, clothes, films and class consciousness. There was going to be a new morality, a new way of living and of loving, a new language. There was going to be fun and experimentation – and it was all going to belong to the young. After all, as a 'typical '60s teenager' interviewed in *Queen* predicted, 'I expect I'll be dead by the time I'm thirty. We all will.'[8]

It didn't happen all at once – sometimes the old ways seemed a long time in dying, and many of them proved to be startlingly resistant – but a culture of opposition, of mould-breaking and anarchism had been gathering force since the mid-1950s. It was iconoclasm running a parallel commentary to affluence – and granted licence by it.

In May 1956 a play opened at the Royal Court Theatre in Sloane Square. *Look Back in Anger* was a rage against class (upper). It was the first play of John Osborne, the 26-year-old grandson of a South London publican, 'a tough, sly old Cockney…who knows how to beat the bailiffs and the money lenders'.[9] It was shocking in its vehemence and it was electrifying. Its 'kitchen sink' style of realist drama, set where an ironing board was the central prop, was also just about as far removed as possible from the theatrical conventions and commercial imperatives of Terence Rattigan's plays, which could not 'displease Aunt Edna' – Rattigan's own 1953 characterization of the 'hopeless lowbrow' whose undiscerning tastes no playwright could afford to disregard.[10] The *Observer*'s theatre critic, Kenneth Tynan (who was

himself a 'wonder boy'[11] of just under thirty), thundered applause for a play that portrays 'post-war youth as it really is, the instinctive leftishness, the surrealist sense of humour…the casual promiscuity, the sense of lacking a cause worth fighting for…the Porters [Jimmy Porter was the anti-hero of the piece] deplore the tyranny of "good taste"…they are "classless".'[12] Two years earlier Tynan had demanded, 'the theatre must widen its scope, broaden its horizon…we need plays about cabmen and demi-gods, plays about warriors, politicians and grocers (as opposed to being about the inhabitants of country houses in Loamshire (or Berkshire)…"which might have been written at any time during the last thirty years")… I counsel aggression because, as a critic, I had rather be a war correspondent than a necrologist.'[13]

It was not just in the theatre that the battle lines were being drawn up, and it was not only John Osborne who was labelled an Angry Young Man – though his spleen lasted for decades. As Tynan reported from the front line, 'The ivory tower has collapsed for good. The lofty, lapidary, "mandarin" style of writing has been replaced by prose that has its feet on the ground… Britain's angry young men may be jejune and strident, but they are involved in the only belief that matters: that life begins tomorrow.'[14]

There was Colin Wilson, an AYM (though this was a media label rather than a movement), an auto-didact, a 'speculative philosopher'[15] in a rather scruffy roll-necked sweater, who kept body and soul together by washing up in coffee bars, working as a hospital porter and claimed to sleep on Hampstead Heath, since that was near enough to the British Museum to enable him to read avidly for his philosophical odyssey, *The Outsider*, published to great acclaim in the same month that *Look Back in Anger* opened.

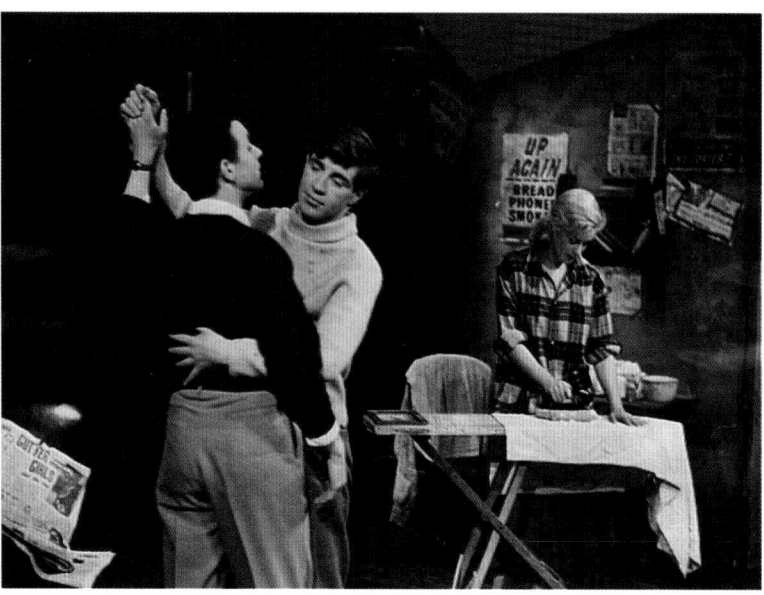

Above
THE EMPTINESS OF
AFFLUENCE
Look Back in Anger,
which opened at the
Royal Court Theatre in
1956 starring Alan Bates,
Kenneth Haigh and Mary
Ure, was a diatribe
against class, the 'posh'
Sunday papers – and
nothingness. 'There
aren't any good, brave
causes left.'

'He's a major writer and he's only twenty-four' ran one headline. Cyril Connolly, the *Sunday Times* critic, found Wilson's treatise on the existential condition of Nietzsche, Blake, Kierkegaard, T.E. Lawrence, Sartre, Van Gogh, Nijinsky and others – people who were 'too clever for the niche to which they were assigned' (which is how Wilson felt about himself) – 'one of the most remarkable books I have read for a long time',[16] while Philip Toynbee, writing in the *Observer*, thought it was 'luminously intelligent'.

There was John Wain, who was twenty-eight when his *Hurry on Down*, a picaresque account of Charles Lumley's deliberate rejection of his middle-class background and education, was published in 1953. Wain (who was to become professor of poetry at Oxford in the 1970s) had no desire to 'stay in permanent opposition' (indeed his publishers issued Wain's books with a disclaimer: 'John Wain is not an Angry

Young Man'[17]), but thought that there was 'one thing worse – permanent conformity' and recognized that 'western mankind' was in 'the position of an inexpert tightrope walker, who has launched himself with a slithering rush, and now finds himself halted with a sea of upturned faces below him, and the second half of his journey still to go'. He demanded that the writer had a right to insist of his public that 'they meet him half-way by making the effort of discrimination'.[18]

There was a young (thirty-four) Swansea university lecturer, Kingsley Amis, whose novel *Lucky Jim* (also published in 1956) was about an outsider too, Jim Dixon, who was 'isolated in enemy territory, making faces to signal that these people were idiots'. But Amis too declined to be labelled an AYM, insisting that he was 'only trying to write a funny novel, while having a few knocks at groups of people I disliked, people who are entrenched in power through no merit of their own'.[19] And in reviewing *The Outsider*, Amis observed that 'one of the prime indications of the sickness of mankind in the mid-twentieth century is that so much excited attention is paid to books about the sickness of mankind in the mid-twentieth century'.[20]

There was Joe Lampton, a working-class boy on the make, who wanted all that money could buy and the boss's daughter too, 'an Aston-Martin, 3-guinea linen shirts, a girl with a Riviera suntan' – the anti-hero of John Braine's novel set in industrial Yorkshire, *Room at the Top*, which was published in 1957 when Braine was thirty-five.

There were other books by young writers that were resolutely unescapist and far from 'Loamshire' (as Tynan called the middle-England which had been the standard setting for British films and plays until the late 1950s); these dealt with the 'realities' of life at the tough end – often in the

Left and below
BRITISH CINEMA
REALISM?
Tom Courtney and
Leonard Rossiter in *Billy
Liar*, a 1963 film scripted
by Keith Waterhouse from
his own novel. It tells the
story of a Walter Mitty-
like character whose
flamboyant fantasies
transform his drab north
country life on the eve of
the 'swinging sixties'.
Tony Richardson's 1961
film version of Shelagh
Delaney's *A Taste of
Honey* (below) starring
(left to right) Rita
Tushingham, Robert
Stephens, Murray Melvin
and Dora Bryan caught in
an archetypal 'New
British Cinema' *verité* of
grimy streets and limited
outlooks.

'When battle is joined one can only hope that blood is drawn'

industrial North or Midlands. Many of these were made into films (*Look Back in Anger* and *Lucky Jim* were both highly successful film adaptations too), in which grainy black-and-white footage panned over grime-, soot- and smoke-belching factory chimneys: *A Taste of Honey* (1957) was written by a seventeen-year-old factory-worker from Salford, Shelagh Delaney, and was filmed with Rita Tushingham as a pregnant Manchester lass; Arthur Seaton was the frustrated Nottingham bicycle-factory worker, who drank and womanized his way through Alan Sillitoe's *Saturday Night and Sunday Morning* (1959), which starred Albert Finney (who had been advised when he went to RADA that, unless he got rid of his northern accent, there would be no parts for him to play). The rallying cry of Arthur, 'Don't let the bastards grind you down', became advice seized upon by the young in the 1960 film version. *Billy Liar* (1959) was the

story of a Yorkshire Walter Mitty character, written by the Leeds journalist Keith Waterhouse and filmed starring Tom Courteney and Julie Christie. And Stan Barstow, a Yorkshire miner's son, wrote a novel entitled *A Kind of Loving* (1960), about Vic Brown trapped by the narrow morality of a lower-middle class 1950s' Britain, filmed with Alan Bates as Vic.

But the youthful critics of society and of the political system had another weapon in their locker to bring out in the late 1950s: satire. In a deferential age, when respect was expected to be paid to position, status, class and age, irreverent humour lit a fuse that was to smoulder and ignite throughout the 1960s. 'When battle is joined one can only hope that blood is drawn,' wrote Jonathan Miller, one of the four young men who had met as undergraduates at Cambridge and devised a revue, *Beyond the Fringe* ('Fringe' because it had been playing on the 'fringe' of the official

Gerald Scarfe.

Edinburgh Festival), which opened at the Fortune Theatre in London on 10 May 1961. In a series of sketches, Dudley Moore at the piano pastiched the styles of Schubert and the collaboration between Benjamin Britten and Peter Pears; the schoolmasterly Alan Bennett from Leeds gave a rendition of a vicar's sermon on the text 'My brother Esau is a hairy man, but I am a smooth man'; Jonathan Miller soliloquized on the meaning of the instructions in railway lavatories – did 'Gentlemen raise the seat' mean a social observation, or a toast? – while in the most hard-hitting of the sketches Peter Cook parodied Harold Macmillan as an old and decaying Prime Minister attempting to converse with the young, dynamic J.F. Kennedy – and then absent-mindedly tearing up a letter he had received from an old-age pensioner.[21]

The next year the *Beyond the Fringe* team – and other satirists like John Wells, John Fortune and Eleanor Bron – moved to a club named after the target of satire's attack, the 'Establishment', housed in a former strip-joint in Greek Street, Soho. Here the late-night revues were more bitingly political and taunting, challenging taboos about sex, the Church, social attitudes and politics – 'all the adornments of a self-confident ruling class were treated as suitable subjects for ribald humour'.[22] The US comedian Lenny Bruce appeared at the 'Establishment', once. His act was judged too lewd for British audiences and he was twice deported by the authorities when he next attempted to entertain at the club.

In November 1962 satire came to television with an entirely disrespectful weekly magazine programme of (fairly) topical satire created and produced by Ned Sherrin, written by David Frost, Christopher Booker and Willie Rushton and starring them (with Frost's transatlantic 'thank you and goodnight' seeming to epitomize classless, confident youth),

Above
THE ESTABLISHMENT
Gerald Scarfe's 1963 cartoon for *Private Eye* of the Establishment Club, which makes the point that whilst pimps, ponces, pornographers and seedy sexual display were permissible in Soho, the US comedian Lenny Bruce, who George Melly welcomed as the 'evangelist of the New Morality', was banned from repeating his 'sick' act at the Establishment which had packed out the house for three weeks in April 1962.

**Above
'THAT WAS THE WEEK
THAT WAS'**
The BBC's short-lived
satirical show which ran
in 1962, commenting on
the week's news with,
from nearest the camera,
David Frost, William
Rushton, Al Mancini, Irwin
Watson, Kenneth Cope
and David Kernan.
Millicent Martin also sang.

with Millicent Martin and Lance Percival; there were guest appearances by, among others, Kenneth Tynan and the barrister/playwright John Mortimer. *That Was the Week That Was* (TW3) almost immediately became unmissable Saturday-night viewing and audience figures rose to an unprecedented twelve million. There were complaints about bad taste and threats to take it off the air, but Harold Macmillan, who was often the butt of its cruellest jokes, stayed the hand of the Postmaster-General when he threatened to intervene.

Another satirical organ, this time in print medium, *Private Eye*, had first hit the bookstalls in October 1961 – but not those stalls owned by W.H. Smith, which refused to stock the scurrilous lampoon. First written and edited by men who had met as schoolboys at Shrewsbury, it all seemed part of the same 'satire circuit' that embraced *Beyond the Fringe* and the 'Establishment'. *Private Eye* cost sixpence a copy for stapled sheets that were left in piles in the burgeoning bistros and coffee bars of Chelsea and Kensington, with an 'honesty' box beside them, whose invariable emptiness – despite the diminishing pile – seemed to bear out Peter Cook's observation 'there is a place in society for nasty-minded, rude people'.[23] *Private Eye*, with its masthead parodying Beaverbrook's *Daily Express* 'Empire crusader', but in this incarnation with a bent and useless sword, was a mixture of public-schoolboy scatological humour, private vilification and debunking those in high – or at least public – places. The Establishment, according to *Private Eye*, comprised politicians, royalty, the Church, the legal profession – and those wearing the striped shirts of consumer affluence. It was a form of snobbish anarchism, where the mere mention of Neasden seemed hilarious, but its targets were well set up for an increasingly self-confident metropolis.

In 1957 an article written by the then Lord Altrincham (who later renounced his title to become plain John Grigg) criticized the Queen in personal terms as 'a priggish schoolgirl, captain of a hockey team, a prefect and recent candidate for confirmation' whose 'style of speaking is frankly a pain in the neck', and who had received a 'woefully inadequate training', which he blamed on the 'people of the tweedy sort, a tight little enclave of English ladies and gentlemen', who surrounded and advised the Royal Family.

The loyal response was immediate: Altrincham was sacked from the *Observer*, for which he wrote, and was assaulted by a member of the League of Empire Loyalists, who was fined £1 for the offence by a magistrate who would clearly have liked to have done the same himself. But Altrincham's views found support from another young aristocrat, the nineteen-year-old Lord Londonderry, in a letter that he wrote to the *New Statesman*. Londonderry was immediately despatched to an Outward Bound school – the extended equivalent of a cold shower – and his noble grandmother, the Dowager Lady Londonderry, explained that he was 'young for his age' and thus 'vulgar...silly...and childish'. Then Malcolm Muggeridge, who might have deserved one but clearly neither of the other two epithets, and who had already coined the expression 'The Royal Soap Opera' in the *New Statesman* two years earlier, joined in with an article published in the American *Saturday Evening Post*, asking 'Does England Really Need a Queen?' Though his rather mild remarks were misquoted, the Establishment closed ranks and Muggeridge was banned from appearing on the BBC.

The most virulent attack came, unsurprisingly, from that class-scourge John Osborne, who declared his contempt for 'that fabulous family we all love so well – the Amazing Windsors! My objection to the Royalty symbol is that it is

ROMANTIC ENGLAND

Above
PRIVATE EYE,
SEPTEMBER 1963
The 'man on the Clapham omnibus' looks on anxiously as rapacious, drunken cavorting holds up his progress. An oblique comment from Willie Rushton on the Profumo affair when it seemed clear that it was the Establishment who were running amok.

dead; it is the gold filling in a mouthful of decay.'[24] Yet while Osborne, Altrincham and others had criticized the Queen for snobbish out-of-touchness, others took a more Bagehotian position, seeing the 'Royal Family' (tabloidese for the monarchy) as being irredeemably (lower) middle-class in their lifestyle and attitudes, and christened the Queen, Brenda and Prince Philip, Brian. However, it rather looked as if the royal critics were nearer to the popular mood than the Establishment liked to imagine, not sharing the media's idolatry towards all persons royal. The *Daily Mail*, which was extremely pro-royal, conducted a poll among its readers and found that 55 per cent of them agreed with Altrincham's criticism of the Court.[25]

There was a gradual unfreezing, or democratization of the monarchy subsequently: the Queen agreed to give her after-lunch Christmas broadcast live on television (and as there were no autocues in those days, this meant that she had to learn the speech off by heart[26]); she went to see a performance of *Beyond the Fringe* and was observed to be amused; the custom of presenting débutantes at Court, a tradition since 1786, ceased in 1958. However, debs did not become extinct: they continued to have dances, serve as a frontispiece to *Country Life* and aim to secure a suitable husband – even though *Queen* promised its readers four years later that 'Débutantes are very different from what they used to be. They are no longer gauche balloons bursting out of tired white tulle crinolines…these young creatures are mostly interested in things outside the "season", in getting a job and making a contribution'; it showed a selection, photographed by Cecil Beaton, to 'show their individuality' – though no actual jobs were mentioned.[27]

Indeed, this same Royal Family, found itself incorporated into the first of the 'swinging London' articles, written by an

American journalist in London for the *Weekend Telegraph* in 1965. 'Much of the stuffiness has been knocked out of the Royal entertaining. The Queen's party for Princess Alexandra and Angus Ogilvy was a really swinging affair that went on to the wee hours… Those used to be dreary affairs. Not long ago Prince Charles and Princess Anne gave a twist and shake party for their young friends at Windsor Castle. Princess Margaret is usually found with actors, writers or painters rather than Guards officers.'[28] This was just as well, since Princess Margaret, the most nonconformist royal, who had been strongly pressured to 'be mindful of the Church's teaching and conscious of my duty to the Commonwealth', did not marry her father George VI's divorced equerry and family friend, Group Captain Peter Townsend, in 1955, but married out in 1960, choosing for herself that most fashionable of figures, a photographer, Anthony Armstrong-Jones, whose work appeared for *Vogue* and *Queen* and who had a studio in the East End.

John Wells had written about the cast of *Beyond the Fringe*, 'we really began to believe that we were, in some sense, the underminers and detonators of politicians'.[29] In the summer of 1963 the explosion came. The press provided the tripwire and the fall-out effectively brought down the Conservative government and revealed how deep were the divisions in British society between the Establishment and its detractors, between the old hypocrisies and a new morality, between the old and the young.

In March 1963 *Private Eye* published a spoof of Gibbon's *Decline and Fall of the Roman Empire* entitled 'The last days of Macmillan', written by Christopher Booker: 'by the early days of the year 1963, the twilight of the British Empire provided a sorry spectacle of collapse and decay on every hand… A strange mood walked abroad in Britain of that year, the eighth of the reign of the Emperor Macmillan. The ability and desire of the Emperor and his advisers to undertake the proper responsibilities of government seem to have quite evaporated…it was in Londinium, at the very heart of the Empire, that rumour, distrust and corruption had finally broken out into the open. After years of an uneasy indulgence, the people were restless and dissatisfied – a spirit which reached into all quarters of society… After his final defeat in the Gallic campaign, after the prolonged and tiring battle of Brussels upon which all his ambitions had been centred [a reference to De Gaulle's veto of Britain's membership of the European Common Market that year], the Emperor Macmillan himself lounged increasingly powerless at the heart of this drift and decay… Wild rumours flew nightly through the capital. Of strange and wild happenings in country villas out in the country. Of orgies and philanderings involving some of the richest and most powerful men in the land… But while natural debauchery became the small talk of a capital long sated with public offerings of vice and harlotry of every description, among the clerks and eunuchs of the administration the old standards of the Republic had vanished altogether. Men proclaimed their love not for their wives, but for each other – and the strange loyalties thus formed, stretching up into some of the highest places in the land, allowed laxity, indulgence and even treason to flourish unchecked.

'At this time too, the Chief of the Praetorian Guard, Sextus Profano, came under widespread suspicion for his admission in the Senate that he had been acquainted with Christina, a beautiful girl known well to many of the great figures of society despite her lowly origins… All these happenings brought the capital into a frenzy of speculation that was far from healthy for the continued reign of

SCANDAL

Macmillan, and the scribes and pamphleteers were only the leaders and articulators of the widespread hostility and contempt aroused by the Government in the hearts of the great mass of the people.'[30]

This was the first reference that *Private Eye* had made to what came to be known as 'the Profumo affair', although rumours were rife in the capital – at least among the media, which had a story they could not print. In July 1961 the Secretary of State for War, John Profumo, had gone to Lord Astor's country seat, Cliveden, with his wife, the actress Valerie Hobson. There, splashing in the swimming pool, he met nineteen-year-old Christine Keeler, who was staying with Stephen Ward, who rented a cottage in the grounds. Ward was a 'society osteopath', who further assisted his clients by introducing them to what were known at the time as 'popsies'. Subsequently Profumo and Keeler had a brief affair.

However, one of Ward's other friends, who also enjoyed the favours of Keeler, was Captain Ivanov, an attaché at the Soviet embassy in London, and a supposed KGB spy. In 1962, at the height of the Cuban missile crisis – when it looked as if the USSR and US were bound on a collision course for nuclear war – the rather unstable Ward determined that he must broker world peace: he offered his services – and connections with Ivanov – to the Foreign Office, which declined them. It was clearly ill-advised for Profumo, as Minister for War, to get too friendly with a man who was so close to what was perceived as the enemy, and the Security Services had cautioned him about his friendship with Ward at the end of 1961: they did not know about Keeler, but this was when Profumo ended his brief relationship with her.

At the beginning of 1963 one of Christine Keeler's ex-lovers, Johnny Edgecombe, fired shots at the house of the

friend she was visiting, 'Mandy' Rice-Davies, in Wimpole Mews. He was charged and Keeler was to be the chief witness for the prosecution. By now an anxious – and broke – Keeler was beginning to talk about her liaison with Profumo, and by March these stories were common currency in *le tout* London: it was then that *Private Eye* published its nearly *en clair* report. The *Sunday Pictorial* agreed to pay Keeler for her story and the Attorney-General confronted Profumo with the allegations, which he vehemently denied. Then, on the eve of the Edgecombe trial, Keeler disappeared and rumours abounded that she had been paid to do so to avoid possible further embarrassment for the Minister. The *Sunday Pictorial* decided that the story was too hot to handle and pulled it, but George Wigg, a Labour MP and a bloodhound on defence matters who had known about the scandal for some time, brought the issue to the floor of the House, demanding that the Home Secretary either deny the rumours that were circulating or set up a Select Committee to inquire into them.

The next day Profumo made a personal statement to the Commons in which he denied any 'impropriety whatsoever in my acquaintanceship with Miss Keeler'. He subsequently successfully sued two continental magazines for repeating the allegations. But by now the police were investigating the affairs of Stephen Ward, and the Prime Minister promised Wigg that he would instigate an inquiry into the possible security aspects of the Ward-Ivanov connection. Profumo, realizing that the game was up, resigned in a letter to the Prime Minister on 5 June 1963, admitting that he had 'misled you, my colleagues and the House of Commons'. 'What the hell is going on in this country?' screamed the *Daily Mirror* headline, as politics went into frenzied overdrive: Labour members wanted to know if Macmillan had been aware that Profumo had lied, and if not why not?

And why was he so out of control of his party, and out of touch with the country? Lord Hailsham went into an unseemly spasm of moral rectitude on television, pontificating about 'dingy companions, squalid vices' and 'a woman of easy virtue'. It was considered that Profumo might in some way contaminate the Queen, were he to return his seals of office personally, so he was required to put them in the post; Christine Keeler was sent to prison for nine months for perjury at the trial of a former lover, Aloysius 'Lucky' Gordon; Stephen Ward was charged with living off the immoral earnings of Keeler and Rice-Davies, and was found guilty, but before he could be sentenced he had killed himself, leaving fourteen suicide notes, maintaining that the charges that he took money for procuring girls were 'a tissue of lies', and apologizing for 'disappointing the vultures'. At his funeral dozens of white roses were sent with a card that read, 'In memory of a victim of British hypocrisy'.

And Macmillan faced his critics in the Commons. It was a humiliating experience, which members of the public had queued all night to behold (most did not get in). Harold Wilson, who had been Leader of the Opposition for only four months (Hugh Gaitskell had died unexpectedly at the age of fifty-six in January) charged the Prime Minister with 'indolent nonchalance' and the Conservatives with being unfit to govern. When Macmillan rose to reply, he admitted not to complicity but to not having known; he confessed that he 'found it difficult to tell the House what a blow it has been to me, for it seems to have undermined one of the very foundations upon which political life must be conducted'. And he made a telling remark when explaining why he had not considered that a letter Profumo had written to Keeler, which began 'Darling', was necessarily evidence of intimacy, saying, 'I do not live among young people much myself.'

Facing page
'HE WOULD, WOULDN'T HE?'
Mandy Rice-Davies and Christine Keeler in July 1963, leaving the trial of the osteopath, Stephen Ward, who was accused of living on their immoral earnings. The above phrase was the response of Rice-Davies when told that Lord Astor had denied her allegations. The phrase resonated in the '60s, much as the phrase 'economical with the truth' did in the '90s.

Above
**VIDAL SASSOON
HAIRCUT**
Vidal Sassoon's famous
geometric cut relied on
sculptured expert cutting
and glossy hair. It was a
style that complemented
the fashion for mini-skirts
and skinny rib jumpers
and was light years away
from the weekly shampoo
and set on rollers, or
teased and lacquered
beehives that had been
the preceding fashion in
hair styles.

Determined not to be brought down 'by two tarts', as he saw them, Macmillan survived – at least until October, when he resigned on grounds of ill-health to be succeeded by a compromise candidate, the patrician 14th Earl of Home, who disarmingly confessed to coming to grips with the nation's economy by counting matchsticks. The satirists had lost their finest target and on *That Was the Week That Was* Willie Rushton sang 'The Party's Over' in a melancholic voice.[31]

'It's young at the top in Washington,' carolled *Queen* in March 1961 about 'the Kennedy style' in US politics, in a story that showed 'young Mr Kennedy' and his close associates in their first week of work in the White House. 'There are three main ingredients. Youth, informality – and plenty of political know-how'.[32] Kennedy had been dead for nearly a year, gunned down by an assassin's bullet in Dallas, Texas, when Harold Wilson's Labour government came to power with a hair's breadth majority of four in October 1964. But Wilson evoked the Kennedy style in his campaign: 'We're going to need something like what President Kennedy had when he came in after years of stagnation…he had a programme of a hundred days – a hundred days of dynamic action.'[33] He talked of 'resurgence' and of an end to nostalgia, the 'grouse-moor' image, out-of-date and backward-looking ways; of 'change…the jet-age, streamlining, modernization, irreverence, and determination'; of automation and space travel; of 'a Socialist-inspired scientific and technological revolution releasing energy on an enormous scale'; and of wanting the youth of Britain, with their 'thrusting ability' and 'iconoclasm', to 'storm the frontiers of knowledge'.

There were new posts as Minister of Technology (first the trade unionist Frank Cousins, and later Anthony Wedgwood

Benn, as he then was) and Minister of Arts (Jennie Lee, Nye Bevan's widow). There was a concentration on education, with the extension of comprehensive education rather than the three-tier grammar, technical and secondary model set up by the 1944 Education Act; and following the Robbins Report of 1963, seven new universities were opened by 1966 (Sussex, East Anglia, Warwick, Essex, York, Kent and Lancaster) and a number of former technical colleges expanded and received university status. With fees paid by local authorities, and student grants, housing and travel allowances available, student numbers increased exponentially, and it really did seem that youth would inherit the earth – bliss it was to be alive in the maelstrom of money, music, fashion, design, drugs and drink that seemed to be their inheritance.

'Youth captured this ancient island and took command in a country where youth had always been kept properly in its place. Suddenly, the young own the town.'[34] The town was London. And at the start of the 1960s the place was the King's Road, though Carnaby Street, a run-down lane at the intersection between Oxford Street and Regent Street, was beginning to jump too, since a Glasgow tailor, John Stephen, had arrived in the capital back in 1953.

Mary Quant was an art student at Goldsmith's College in the 1950s, to whom 'adult appearance was very unattractive, alarming and terrifying, stilted, confined and ugly. It was something I knew I didn't want to grow into. I saw no reason why childhood could not last for ever.'[35] So she started designing her own clothes, pinafores, short skirts, skimpy dresses, 'clothes that allowed people to run, to jump, to leap, to retain their precious freedom'. Quant (and her husband Alexander Plunkett Greene) opened a shop called Bazaar in 1955 to sell their own designs. It immediately became the

Above
BAZAAR
'If we could find the right premises for a boutique in the King's Road...we would call it Bazaar.' Mary Quant on the shop that revoltionized British fashion.

mary quant

Mary Quant opened her shop, Bazaar, with her husband, Alexander Plunket Greene in 1955.

'There really was a vacuum in those days. There was simply nothing for young people. The older generation were dying to revert to pre-war ways, but...we wanted to go forward, to do something new. The art schools were a great forcing-house of talent not just clothes but music...design, food, lifestyle, politics, everything.

I'd been designing clothes since I was five or six. It's all I ever wanted to do. I loved using new materials like PVC and new combinations like men's suiting, flannel, pinstripes mixed in with feminine fabric like satin and lace.

I just made clothes for the people I knew. I was rather offended at first when US manufacturers started to want to buy my designs! It was very much a Chelsea thing. We all hung out as a group in the King's Road, around the Royal Court and drinking espresso in the Fantasy coffee bar. There was John Osborne, Terence Conran, Elizabeth Frink, Bailey and Donovan. We were all tremendous friends, all pushing out in different directions, but there was a great deal of cross-pollination going on.'

Above
'SUITS EXHIBITED'
A *Good Housekeeping*
feature in September 1964
posed clothes in front of
'60s paintings by such
artists as Roy Lichtenstein
and, in this case, Richard
Anuszkiewicz.

centre of the 'Chelsea Set'. 'Nobody has been able to make up his mind what "the Chelsea Set" was,' Quant admitted, 'but…it grew out of something in the air which developed into a serious effort to break away from the Establishment. It was the first real indication of a complete change of outlook. The fact that this change gathered momentum so much more quickly than anyone ever imagined was unpredictable.'[36]

The King's Road, which had been a street of 'tall plane trees, white-fronted houses and redcoated Chelsea pensioners', where families did their shopping at 'Jones the grocer where there were glass-topped biscuit tins, Timothy Whites, Sidney Smith the drapers, and the Woolworths with its counters piled high with sweets…gradually began to change…suddenly the King's Road was full with new and unlikely people, all of the magical age in which they were adult, but not old. From Bazaar, remarkable at first for the simplicity of its lines, came the mini skirt. This smallest of shops reached fame through the very smallness of its garments. Local residents stared and pointed as young women catwalked up and down the King's Road. The women…wore floppy hats, skinny ribbed sweaters, key-hole dresses, wide hipster belts… They had white lip-sticked lips and thick black eyeliner, hair cut at alarming angles, op-art earrings and ankle-length white boots. They wore citron-coloured trouser suits and skirts that seemed daily shorter. [By 1965 the hem-line was nearing six inches above the knee, though in 1964 the model Jean Shrimpton had caused a scandal in Australia, and a week of headlines back in Britain, when she wore a dress four inches above the knee to the races.] They rode on miniature motorbikes. They had confidence and, it seemed, no parents.'[37]

Vidal Sassoon, a young hairdresser with a salon in Bond Street, cut hair that had previously been 'feminine' and

BIBA

demanding of a weekly shampoo-and-set, or teased it into a stiff, lacquered bouffant beehive, into a gleaming geometric helmet of razor-precise lines that suggested androgyny and independence. Barbara Hulanicki, a fashion artist, opened a tiny boutique in an old chemist's shop in a back street in Abingdon Road, Kensington. She had had great success with her mail-order fashion business, when the *Daily Express* offered 'something cool and shifty…if you think gingham is an "in" fabric…if you like the idea of a headscarf to match…if you feel that twenty-five bob [shillings = £1.25] isn't a fashion fortune'[38] – and had promptly sold 17,000. Biba's two-guinea brown chalkstripe shift – again with matching headscarf – sold out from the boutique. And the art-nouveau style, moody navy-blue walls and gold logos of the shop, staffed by skinny *Ready, Steady, Go* Cathy McGowan wannabes, with their long straight hair and spiky-lashed eyes – which you could not actually see because they were hidden by a fringe – came to define the 1960s. All this and a miasma of hats with holes like Emmenthal cheese, feather boas, grandfather vests, T-shirt dresses and knee-length suede boots, all in dusty, bruised autumn colours like plum and rust, modelled by girls who looked like sexualized children, with their pouty lips, huge kohl-ringed panda eyes and fragile, waif-like posture.

Before the 1960s fashion models had been elegant women, rather grown-up and perfectly groomed, posed in romantic settings – leaning on a pillar, draped round a sundial – and photographed by equally stylish and well-dressed men such as Cecil Beaton and John French. A new breed of photographer now looked for a new object for his lens and for a novel way of imaging that made a photograph into an action picture, which suggested a narrative rather than just a frock being displayed. The East End provided the

Left
BIBA
Sketch of a towelling mini-dress designed by Barbara Hulanicki for her Biba mail-order catalogue in 1964, the year the first Biba shop opened.

Right
JEAN SHRIMPTON
The face of the '60s, Jean Shrimpton (dubbed 'the shrimp' by the press) modelling a 5-guinea Miss Polly dress. Shrimpton was a model 'discovered' when she was 17 by the photographer David Bailey whose pictures shot the leggy model to a fame that proclaimed that it was groovy to be young, girls did not have to dress like their mothers.

visual chroniclers for up West, a Cockney cast that included David Bailey, Terence Donovan and Brian Duffy snapping the new supermodels – the most famous of whom was the colt-like Jean Shrimpton – and even the aristocratic Lord Snowdon's studio was located in Rotherhithe. But the photographers did not just portray the action in grainy black and white: they were the action too. They were where it was at, and celebrity was rewritten. 'There is now a curious cultural community,' wrote Jonathan Miller, 'breathlessly à la mode, where Lord Snowdon and other desperadoes of the grainy layout jostle with commercial art-school Mersey stars, window dressers and Carnaby Street pants-peddlars. Style is the thing here – Taste 64 – a cool line and the witty insolence of youth.'[39]

'Possibly no other society, so small in number, has tattooed its image so indelibly across the face of a whole generation. It was a time of no-deposit, non-returnable, disposable fame…narcissistic, ruthless, often talented, and malignantly ambitious, they were the butterflies born to be broken on the wheel of fashion,' wrote the journalist Francis Wyndham.[40] Yet although 'glamour dates fast, and its ephemeral nature both attracts Bailey and challenges him [as] he tries to capture it on the wing',[41] many of those he photographed on the swinging trapeze of 1960s' style-makers formed a remarkably coherent cohort – and their influence has persisted well beyond that tinsel decade. When Terence Conran (who had designed the Knightsbridge branch of Bazaar) opened his first Habitat shop in May 1964, just along the Fulham Road (which runs parallel to the King's Road) from the first Laura Ashley, the staff were dressed in Mary Quant outfits (and blue-striped butcher's aprons) their hair scissored by Vidal Sassoon.[42] It was a revolution in furniture selling – no more rows of chintz sofas, but rather a

Above
THE WEDDING OF THE DECADE?
Photographer David Bailey, whose photographs had created and captured the mood of the '60s, married the French film actress, Catherine Deneuve (*Les Parapluies de Cherbourg*) in a polo-necked sweater at St Pancras Town Hall on 18 August 1965, with Mick Jagger as best man. The marriage did not survive the decade.

Left
DARLING
Julie Christie in John Schlesinger's *Darling* (1965) 'a fashionable mid-sixties concoction of smart swinging people and their amoral doings', which, despite its vacuity, became an influential stereotype of the '60s.

'It was a revolution in furniture selling – no more rows of chintz sofas, but rather a "complete home concept"'

Above
HABITAT
The first Habitat shop opened on the corner of the Fulham Road in May 1964. It was, eulogized *House Beautiful* ('the magazine for young homemakers') 'almost worth coming to town to see' with a range that stretched from 'a 6d set of wooden skewers...to an Arne Jacobsen chair'. And what was more 'their taste is not entirely motivated by Swedish design and "what's good from abroad". After more than a year's thorough search more than two thirds of their stock is British'.

'complete home concept' of modern design. The walls were unplastered, painted brick, and the merchandise, which was massed on the shelves rather than taking the usual 'sample' approach to shopping at the time, came from all over the world – Magistretti painted wood and rush chairs from Italy, Japanese paper lampshades, pale blond pine from Scandinavia, and the cookery utensils and tableware, from chicken bricks and butcher's blocks to earthenware casseroles, that were required to realize Elizabeth David's robust French peasant cooking.

Like clothes, popular music began to traduce all accepted conventions in the mid-1950s: it no longer dealt in harmony and syncopation; its lyrics were no longer the perky repetitions of groups like the Platters, or sentiment-to-sway-to from the likes of Perry Como, Frank Sinatra, Frankie Vaughan or Rosemary Clooney, but louder and more

urgent, subversive, puzzling and not a little disturbing to an older generation.

In 1955, the same year that youth's symbol of living fast and dying young, James Dean, was killed in a car crash (and, when the twisted wreck of his Porsche went on show, 800,000 kids went to see it, and for three years after his violent end sent fanmail of 2,000 letters a week refusing to believe their idol was dead[43]), a new film about discontented and violent US teenagers, *The Blackboard Jungle*, was released in Britain. Its accompanying soundtrack, 'Rock Around the Clock', was belted out by a little-known group, Bill Haley and the Comets. Its effect in Britain was electrifying: it was as if it provided an outlet for years of post-war frustration and quietude. Young cinema-goers – 'rhythm-crazed youngsters'[44] – got up and jived in the aisles as soon as the first raucous notes were heard; seats were razored; and

fights broke out between police and the mainly young motorcyclists with leather jackets and greasy cow's-lick hair: a younger generation of an earlier phenomenon, the Teddy Boy, who had appropriated – and exaggerated – the formal dress of the English upper classes of the beginning of the century.

It was a style that had been revived in the early 1950s by Savile Row, but it was not the sartorially aware of the West End who had donned it, but the young, largely working class of London – particularly east and south London – who dressed in Edwardian-style 'draped' jackets, tight drainpipe trousers, bootlace ties and thick crêpe-soled suede 'brothel creepers' or 'beetle crushers', with exaggerated sideburns and their hair greased into a 'DA' (Duck's Arse) quiff. They were the first manifestations of a distinct youth culture and a chasm was riven by their behaviour. 'Tribal' gangs formed,

Left
TEDDY BOY
A 'Teddy Boy', so-called from his adoption of the 'Edwardian' style of dress. This example of the species appeared in *Picture Post* in May 1954 to illustrate an article investigating whether simply dressing like a modified dandy really justified the abuse that was heaped on all teddy boys as 'hooligans, gangsters and juvenile delinquents'.

Above
ROCK AROUND THE CLOCK
'The American rock-and-roll king' whose music whipped British teenagers into a dancing frenzy, Bill Haley and his Comets, rehearsing for the first show of their British tour in February 1957.

peter blake

Peter Blake was a defining artist for the '60s with his paintings which included and the sleeve for the Beatles record 'Sergeant Pepper's Lonely Heart's Club Band' (1967).

'I left the Royal College of Art in 1956 and travelled for a year and then came back to build a career for myself as a painter. I taught too – at St Martin's and Harrow and Walthamstow. You could make a living that way in those days and still have time to paint. So as soon as term finished in 1961 I stood in front of a mirror and started to paint *Self Portrait with Badges*.

I just painted myself in what I was wearing which was denim and baseball boots. That was unusual in those days, people only wore sports clothes for playing sport, and jeans were still considered as workmen's clothes, but that's what I wore, so that's what I painted myself in. I actually didn't have that many badges. Grown men didn't wear badges in those days, and I certainly was not a supporter of Adlai Stevenson, but I had the badge so I included it in the picture. It was the same with the Elvis magazine – I still subscribe to that.

The painting was in the tradition of self-portraiture, like Watteau or Stanley Spencer, a traditional form but in a popular style – the everyday. That's what I wanted to do: I wanted to make enjoying paintings available to ordinary people. It was to be like pop music, accessible and fun.

1961 was a breakthrough year for me. It put pop art on the map. I won the junior prize in the John Moores competition with *Self Portrait*, and then Ken Russell made a film for *Monitor* [a TV arts programme], *Pop Goes the Easel*, and then I was featured again in the first issue of the *Sunday Times* colour supplement.'

'SELF PORTRAIT WITH BADGES' (1961) BY PETER BLAKE. Blake is a figurative painter whose pop art not only makes reference to popular culture idols and ephemera, but was a formative part of that culture.

whose dialogue was often that of the flick-knife or bicycle chain; street furniture was smashed, train and bus seats slashed in a graffiti of violence. 'Teddy' suits were frequently banned from dance halls, their owners often being in trouble with the police and vilified by magistrates, who were called upon to see not only their crimes and misdemeanours, but also their dress, as sure evidence of the decline of a useful – and deferential – generation which, in their oft-stated view, the ending of National Service had done nothing to improve.

But when Bill Haley actually arrived in Britain on tour, 'hoping to dig you British cats' in 1957, the illusion was shattered. Haley was not youth: he was middle-aged, and those 'hep chicks and cats' wanted that loud voice of revolt to be their own age, not nearly that of their parents. Their new idols were home-grown, discovered in the Gaggia-equipped coffee bars of Soho (of which the 'Two i's' in Old Compton

Street was the most famous) – youths like Marty Wilde or the twenty-year-old Tommy Hicks, an ex-sailor from Bermondsey, who renamed himself Tommy Steele and cut a record 'Singing the Blues', which topped the bestsellers chart for three months. There were more renames: Adam Faith, Cliff Richard (whose 'Livin' Doll' written by Lionel Bart, was a platter spun for decades), Billy Fury, Vince Eager.

But, despite the promise of their names, these were homely balladeers, warbling about 'Little White Bulls' (Steele) and 'We're All Going on a Summer Holiday' (Richard) for family entertainment, as were their US counterparts Pat Boone, Nat King Cole, Paul Anka (though theirs were songs about misunderstood-youth-in-love). And then there was Elvis, the snake-hipped sensualist from Tennessee, 'a white boy who can sing coloured', with his croonings of love, longing and, above all, lust – 'Heartbreak

Hotel', 'Jailhouse Rock', 'All Shook Up', 'Blue Suede Shoes', 'Hardhearted Woman' – before he too had to go off to do his National Service (US-style).

There was an intellectual divide about music for the young in the 1950s. Those who despised the anodyne music of the rockers turned to jazz, the music of black America, which sprang in those years from New Orleans and caught the imagination of university students, CND protesters, AYM and their creations. They went to hear 'trad jazz' at Humphrey Lyttleton's club at 100 Oxford Street. George Melly, who sung the Blues pretty persuasively himself, recognized: 'the audience [for jazz] was middle-class and suburban with a strong element of students, particularly from art school. Trad was the music of the Aldermaston marchers. The English rock 'n' roll audience, on the other hand, was mostly working-class and very young… Jazz enthusiasts despised rock 'n' roll as musically illiterate.'[45]

They may have been despised by the minority duffle-coat brigade, but in 1959 British teenagers were spending on average £8 a week (£830 million in total) on clothes, cigarettes, records and cosmetics.[46] It gave them identity and power of a sort, as Colin MacInnes described in his novel of the 1950s, *Absolute Beginners*: 'The teenage ball had a real, savage splendour in the days when we found that no one couldn't sit on our faces any more because we had loot to spend at last and our world was to be our world…'[47] Their music also, symbolically, first came from beyond the airwaves controlled by the BBC, who broadcast only one half-hour programme of pop in the early 1960s. Teenagers retreated to their bedrooms and tuned into the crackling, often fading Radio Luxembourg to hear DJs like Pete Murray and Jimmy Savile dexterously keep up a stream of commentary as they played a continuous sequence of current hits.

In 1964 an enterprising entrepreneur started broadcasting from a ship, the *Caroline*, moored outside the jurisdiction of the British courts. The pirate Radio Caroline soon attracted millions of young listeners, while the Foreign Office complained to the Panamanian government (where the ship was registered) and the Post Office was ordered to isolate the vessel from all mainland communication. But for three years, until it was closed down by law to ensure the safety of the airwaves, bands of pirate ships swarmed across the airwaves, making pop subversive by the very manner of its transmission.

Youth affluence and the musical divide took on more potency in the 1960s in the aggravation between mods and rockers. Rockers liked to straddle macho-fast motorbikes and looked like Hell's Angels, with greasy hair, leather jackets and tattoos; they roared down the motorway terrorizing families on an outing in their Hillman Minx, and congregated at petrol-station cafés, particularly the Ace and the Busy Bee around the Watford terminus of the M1. Mods, who took their name from the Modern Jazz movement (the music of Charlie Mingus and Dave Brubeck), liked to look 'Italian' with their sharp-cut mohair suits, dark sunglasses and neatly coiffeured hair; they rode motor scooters, since they could usually save up their wages to put down a deposit on a 150cc Lambretta for just over £100; and they habituated Soho clubs where they danced to the music of the Yardbirds (and later The Who) after they had watched the compulsory Friday-night viewing of *Ready Steady, Go!* Their dances were the ska,

the shake and they popped Purple Hearts (the drug drinamyl, named after the US medal awarded to those wounded in action), to sustain those weekend marathons.

Mods despised and generally ignored Rockers. But in 1964 during a cold, wet, nothing-much-to-do Easter weekend at Clacton, 1,000 Mods caused havoc among the shut-up cafés and stacked-for-the-season deckchairs, as they fought with Rockers and the police who came to keep order. Every Bank Holiday that summer and the next, south-coast seaside towns within easy reach of London – Margate, Brighton, Bournemouth, Hastings – were invaded by Mods in convoys of pennanted scooters. These towns were 'suddenly full of warring kids, up to their skulls in amphetamine, wrecking the cafés, hunting one another in great bloodthirsty packs across the beach. They didn't even bother to turn off the transistors as they put in the boot.'[48] Fines and custodial sentences of exemplary severity were handed out by local magistrates, who talked of 'filth' and 'pollution'; and there were calls in Parliament for stricter laws against 'malicious damage' and against drugs. But by the end of 1965 youth culture had shifted from this particular distraction, that style, those drugs.

In 1963 the *Evening Standard* came out with a special issue that proclaimed the previous twelve months as 'the Year of the Beatles' – the outstandingly successful Merseyside beat group that had attracted attention in the Cavern Club in Liverpool. Influenced by the black beat of Tamla Motown, Chuck Berry, Fats Domino and Little Richard,[49]

MEET THE

STAR SPECIAL

Number Twelve

BEATLES

AN INFORMAL DATE IN WORDS & PERSONAL ALBUM PICTURES

2'6

INTRODUCED by THEMSELVES

Written and compiled by

TONY BARROW

their records – 'From Me to You', 'She Loves You', 'Can't Buy Me Love', 'I Wanna Hold Your Hand' – dominated the hit parade. 'If you want to know about the Sixties, play the music of the Beatles,' the American composer, Aaron Copland, advised.

By the time they hit the big time under the guidance of Brian Epstein – who took them out of the skiffle gear they had worn while playing in the Hamburg clubs (and, in the case of Lennon and McCartney, in a group known as the Quarry Men) and into lapel-less 'mod' suits and scarab-smooth haircuts – the group of self-taught musicians consisted of John Lennon, Paul McCartney, George Harrison and Ringo Starr (Richard Starkey). The Beatles wrote their own songs (at least three of them did) and then performed them live. The response was Beatlemania, with screaming, fainting fans greeting their every performance and every hoped-for appearance. They sold millions of records, conquered the US, which had held unquestioned musical hegemony since the war, and appealed right across age barriers in a way that the more *outré* and explicit anti-authority, pro-drug experimentation bands like the next big one on the scene, the Rolling Stones, never did; they were awarded the MBE by a fellow-Liverpudlian (Harold Wilson) in 1965, and opined – or John Lennon did – a year later that they were more popular than Jesus Christ. According to *The Times*, the 'fab four' 'enabled millions more to crack the barriers that existed between classes, between London culture and that of the provinces, between Scouse and Geordie and the accents of the BBC and Oxbridge. Their style of dress and hair and their irreverent behaviour led the youth of Britain to a new and independent identity. The Beatles were not the most outrageous or iconoclastic members of the pop scene, but their example was the most influential.'[50]

Facing page
BEATLEMANIA
The "fab four" telling about themselves in words and pictures.

Above
UNDERGROUND
The famous Cavern Club in Liverpool, where the Beatles first attracted media attention.

Left
"TWIST AND SHOUT
Released in March 1963, a version of the US Isley Brother's (a black Cincinnati family) hit of the previous summer.

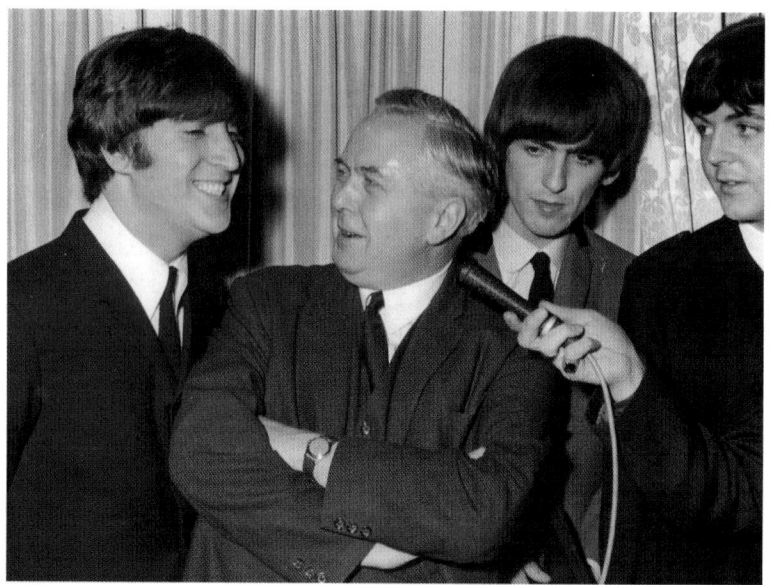

'Everyone dressed up, but nothing changed'

Above
COOL BRITANNIA
The Labour Prime
Minister, Harold Wilson
presents the 'Show
Business of the Year
Award' to the Beatles in
1964. The following year
Wilson awarded them the
MBE which caused howls
of protest from earlier
recipients who regarded
the gesture as a
trivialization of the award.

Facing page
'FOR WHOM THE BELL
TOLLS'
The state funeral of Sir
Winston Churchill on 30
January 1965. 3,000
silent mourners lined the
route as the Union Jack-
draped coffin was carried
on a gun carriage, pulled
by sailors and escorted by
guardsmen, through the
streets of the capital.

Standing as a metaphor for the 1960s, the Beatles were both the 'unacknowledged legislators of populist revolt'[51] and at the same time 'took what the man with the big cigar had to offer'.[52] They fused 'saccharined anarchy saying "Go to Hell" tunefully'[53] with consumerism, and segued towards the end of the decade, embracing all it had to offer in pop art ('Sergeant Pepper's Lonely Hearts Club Band'), drug-induced psychedelia ('Lucy in the Sky with Diamonds'), break-up and finally denunciation of the decade ('Everyone dressed up but nothing changed').[54]

On 24 January 1965, Sir Winston Churchill died aged ninety. The man who had fought in the Boer War and led his country through the second of the century's world wars was honoured with a state funeral, and for two days mourners filed past his flag-draped catafalque in Westminster Hall, because 'Churchill at a certain time and in a special way was,

for all public purposes, Britain and more than Britain.'[55] In 1945 Churchill had announced the coming of peace. Twenty years later, watching his funeral, the journalist Patrick O'Donovan wrote in the *Observer*: 'This was the last time such a thing could happen. This was the last time that London would be the capital of the world... This marked the final act in Britain's greatness.'[56]

In less than three months London was again being hailed as the capital of the world. But it was a different world: the accolade was not for 'Britain's greatness' on the world stage; not for Britain the superpower. It was for a Britain of dynamic youth, of innovation, of popular culture and conspicuous consumption. This was a generation that seemed a lifetime away from that moment in May 1945 when Churchill briefly reaped his reward for Britain's 'finest hour'. The landscape – both physical and mental – was different. The young were in

'Sexual intercourse began in nineteen sixty-three...'

a different country, and were themselves a different country with a new identity, new affluence, new rules for living. Only five years earlier it had been possible for the prosecuting counsel to ask, in the case when Penguin Books tested the meaning of the Obscene Publication Act by publishing an unexpurgated edition of D.H. Lawrence's *Lady Chatterley's Lover* – in numbers and at a price that made it available for almost all, if they wanted it – 'Is this a book that you would wish your wife or servants to read?' It had been impossible to find expert witnesses for the prosecution; for the defence, all 300 people who had been asked to testify (except the Lawrence scholar and educational influence of a generation, F.R. Leavis) agreed that it was. In the event, over a period of six days, seventy witnesses were called upon to vouch not just for the book's literary merit, but, more to the point, for the people's right to read it. This was a marker in the new topography, as Philip Larkin recognized:

> Sexual intercourse began
> In nineteen sixty-three
> (Which was rather late for me) –
> Between the end of the *Chatterley* ban
> And the Beatles' first LP.[57]

There were more revolutions to come: the death penalty was abolished in 1965 – for a trial period, although it has never been reinstated, despite periodic demands; two years later it was no longer a criminal offence for consenting adults over

twenty-one who lived in England or Wales to have a homosexual relationship in private; abortion on social and psychological, as well as medical, grounds was legalized; the contraceptive pill, first developed in the 1950s, became widely available and made reliable birth control the prerogative of women; and by the end of the decade women had started to formulate a systematic and active critique of their own unfreedom. The 'cultural consensus' between the generations had broken down (if it had ever really existed) with the emergence of a politicized underground counter-culture that viewed drugs as their experimental fiefdom. A teenager was first charged with possession of marijuana in 1952; by 1967 there were nearly 2,500 prosecutions. In 1965 the young were taking a hallucinogenic drug known by its initials, in significant numbers – possession of LSD was not made illegal until 1967, and the vivid, swirling fluorescent psychedelic trips it induced produced the graphics of the underground for a decade.

Eight years after *Look Back in Anger*, the anti-hero of John Osborne's play, *Inadmissible Evidence* (first performed in September 1964), was not an angry young man, a terrier at the heels of past values. He was a corrupt solicitor, Bill Maitland, and in the play he rails at his teenage daughter, 'They're young…and for the first time they're being allowed to roll about in it and have clothes and money and music and sex, and you can take or leave any of it. No one before has been able to do such things with such charm, such ease, such frozen innocence as all of you seem to have.' [58]

**Above
'5-4-3-2-1' (1963) BY
PAULINE BOTY.**
The title, after a song by Manfred Mann, echoed the countdown to the pop programme *Ready, Steady, Go*. Boty, who died in 1966, aged 28, was the only woman pop artist, an exuberant and sensual painter with 'a nostalgia for the present', whose work predicted a feminist agenda in the coming decades.

footnotes

THE LAND OF BEGINNING AGAIN

1. Naomi Mitchison, *Among You Taking Notes: The Wartime Diaries of Naomi Mitchison*, 1939–45, ed. Dorothy Sheridan (Oxford: Oxford University Press, 1986) p.320

2. John W. Wheeler-Bennett, *King George VI* (London: Macmillan, 1958) p.624

3. *Harold Nicolson, Diaries and Letters 1939–45,* ed. Nigel Nicolson (London: Fontana, 1970), HN to NN, 8 May 1945, pp.460–1

4. Mitchison, op.cit, p.321

5. David Kendall, *Poems of an Ordinary Seaman* (London: Fortune Press, 1946), quoted in Andrew Sinclair, *War Like a Wasp: The Lost Decade of the Forties* (London: Hamish Hamilton, 1989) p.202

6. James Lansdale Hodson, *The Way Things Are: Being an account of journeys, meetings, and what was said to me in Britain between May 1945 and January 1947* (London: Victor Gollancz, 1947) p.21

7. C.D. Lewis, 'Will it be so again?' from *Collected Poems* (London: Jonathan Cape, 1954)

8. Anthony Howard, 'We are the Masters Now' in Michael Sissons and Philip French (eds), *The Age of Austerity, 1945–1951* (London: Hodder and Stoughton, 1963) p.17

9. Tom Harrisson, *Living Through the Blitz* (London: Collins, 1976) p.316

10. Quoted in Martin Gilbert, *Never Despair. Winston S. Churchill 1945–1965* (London: Heinemann, 1988) p.111

11. Harold Nicolson's report of a conversation with Robin Maugham, Nicolson, op. cit., 10 August 1945, p.32

12. Quoted in Peter Hennessy, 'The Attlee Government, 1945–51' in Peter Hennessy and Anthony Seldon (eds), *Ruling Performances. British Governments from Attlee to Thatcher* (Oxford: Blackwell, 1987) p.32. Hennessy says that he first heard this possibly apocryphal story from Sir Robin Day.

13. *Social Insurance and Allied Services* (London: HMSO, 1942) p.6. Quoted in Peter Hennessy, *Never Again. Britain 1945–51* (London: Jonathan Cape, 1992) p.67

14. R.B. McCallum and Alison Readman, *The British General Election of 1945* (Oxford: Oxford University Press, 1947) p.150, footnote 1

15. *Demobilisation in Britain* (Central Office of Information, 1 May 1947)

16. Quoted in Harry Hopkins, *The New Look: A Social History of the Forties and Fifties* (London: Secker and Warburg, 1964) p.15

17. Hodson, op. cit., 17 August 1945, p.22

18. Quoted in Barry Turner and Tony Rennell, *When Daddy Came Home: How Family Life Changed Forever in 1945* (London: Hutchinson, 1995) p.19

19. Christopher Hassall, 'Hats, demob depot, York' from *The Slow Night* (London: Arthur Barker, 1949)

20. Sinclair, op. cit., p.200

21. Mrs Winnie Whitehouse, quoted in Paul Addison, *Now the War is Over. A Social History of Britain, 1945–51* (London: Jonathan Cape, 1985; Pimlico edition with new introduction, 1995)

22. Lord Woolton, Diary for 1 November 1940, quoted in Addison, op. cit., p.55

23. Ibid., p.58

24. Deborah S. Ryan, *The Ideal Home Through the 20th Century* (London: Hazar Publishing, 1997) p.88

25. Ibid., p.87

26. Ibid., p.92

27. Hodson, op. cit., pp.24–5

28. Susan Cooper, 'Snoek Piquante' in Sissons and French (eds), op. cit., p.35

29. Ibid., pp.35–6

30. Ibid., p.38

31. Ibid., p.43

32. Alex J. Robertson, *The Bleak Midwinter: 1947* (Manchester: Manchester University Press, 1987) p.21

33. Cyril Connolly, *Horizon*, 1947

34. Ibid., p.56

35. Quoted in Fiona MacCarthy, *All Things Bright and Beautiful. Design in Britain, 1830 to Today* (London: Allen and Unwin, 1972) p.145

36. Ibid., p.145

37. Ibid., p.146

38. David Hughes, 'The Spivs' in Sissons and French, op. cit., pp.86–105

39. Ibid., pp.101–2

40. Ibid, pp. 99–100

41. Virginia Graham, 'A Thought for Denman Street' from *Consider the Years, 1938–1946* (London: Jonathan Cape, 1947)

42. Ross McKibben, *Classes and Cultures in England 1918–1951* (Oxford: Oxford University Press, 1998) p.419

43. Robert Hewison, *In Anger: Culture in the Cold War, 1945–60* (London: Weidenfeld and Nicolson, 1981) p.8

44. See Chapter 5, 'Living It Up', in Addison, op. cit., pp.113–39

45. Quoted in Pearson Phillips 'The New

Look', ibid., pp.133–4

THE ATOMIC AGE

1. Ian Cox, *The South Bank Exhibition: A Guide to the Story it Tells* (London: HMSO, 1951) p.6
2. Ibid.
3. *Harold Nicolson, Diaries and Letters, 1945–1962* (London: Collins, 1968) p.206
4. Michael Frayn, 'Festival' in Sissons and French, *The Age of Austerity*, p.343
5. Max Nicholson, a temporary civil servant in Morrison's department, quoted in Addison, *Now the War is Over*, p.207
6. Frayn, op. cit., p.331
7. Ibid., p.336
8. Ibid. (quoting Gerald Barry), p.336
9. MacCarthy, *All Things Bright and Beautiful*, p.173
10. Victor Passmore, 'A Jazz Mural' in Mary Banham and Bevis Hillier (eds), *A Tonic to the Nation: The Festival of Britain, 1951* (London: Thames and Hudson, 1976) p.102
11. Misha Black, 'Architecture, Art and Design in Unison', ibid., p.83
12. Margaret Sheppard Fidler, 'Naming the Skylon', ibid., p.168
13. Cox, op. cit., p.9
14. Ibid., p.12
15. Ibid., p.8
16. Ibid., p.4
17. MacCarthy, op. cit., pp.173–4
18. Hugh Casson, 'Period Piece' in *A Tonic to the Nation: The Festival of Britain, 1951* (London, Thames and Hudson, 1976) pp. 76–81
19. R.D. Russell, Robert Godden, 'The Lion and the Unicorn Pavilion' in Banham and Hillier, op. cit., p.96
20. 'Battersea Pleasures', interview with James Gardner, ibid., p.121
21. *Festival of Britain*, 1951
22. Adrian Forty, 'Festival Politics' in

Banham and Hillier, op. cit., p.38
23. William Feaver, 'Festival Star', ibid., p.40
24. Ibid., p.65
25. Ibid., pp.65–6
26. Ibid., p.66
27. Ibid.
28. Arthur Marwick, *British Society since 1945* (Harmondsworth: Penguin, third edition 1996)
29. Sally MacDonald and Julia Porter, *Putting on the Style: Setting Up Home in the 1950s* (London: The Geffrye ` Museum, 1990) unnumbered pages
30. Quoted in Lesley Jackson, *The New Look. British Design in the 1950s* (London: Thames and Hudson, 1998) p.85
31. Ibid., p.87
32. Polly Powell and Lucy Peel, *'50s and '60s Style* (London: Grange Books, 1994) pp.22–3
33. 'The Story the Exhibition Tells' in Banham and Hillier, op. cit., p.144
34. Jackson, op. cit., pp.90–1
35. Roger Sabin, *Adult Comics: An Introduction* (London: Routledge, 1993) pp.25–6
36. Jackson, op. cit., p.92
37. Michael Dockrill, 'Britain in the Nuclear Age' in Terry Gourvish and Alan O'Day (eds), *Britain Since 1945* (Basingstoke: Macmillan, 1991) p.139
38. Peter Lewis, *The Fifties* (London: William Heinemann, 1978) p.88
39. Christopher Pearce, *Fifties Source Book* (New York: Chartwell Books Inc., 1990) p.135
40. See William Wallace, 'World Status Without Tears' in Vernon Bogdanor and Robert Skidelsky (eds), *The Age of Affluence, 1951–1964* (Basingstoke: Macmillan, 1980)
41. Quoted in Anne Deighton, *The Impossible Peace: Britain, the Division of Germany and the Cold War* (Oxford: Clarendon Press, 1990) p.186

42. Franks to Attlee, 15 July 1950, quoted in Hennessy, *Never Again*, p.404
43. Quoted in Lewis, op. cit., p.66
44. Nicolson, op. cit., 8 June 1951
45. Goronwy Rees quoted in Martin Green, *Children of the Sun* (London: Constable, 1977) p.430
46. Richard Hoggart, *A Sort of Clowning: Life and Times, Volume II 1940–59* (London: Chatto and Windus, 1990) pp.198–9
47. Keith Middlemass, *Power, Competition and the State, Volume I. Britain in Search of Balance, 1940–61* (Basingstoke: Macmillan, 1988) p.116
48. A factory worker, quoted in Peter Chambers and Amy Landreth (eds), *Called Up: The Personal Experience of 16 National Servicemen by Themselves* (London: Allan Wingate, 1955)
49. Dockrill, op. cit., p.141
50. Sidney Pollard, *The Wasting of the British Economy* (London: Croom Helm, 1984) p.37
51. Dockrill, op. cit., p.137
52. Quoted in Alistair Horne, *Macmillan*, vol. II(Basingstoke: Macmillan, 1989) p.50
53. C.M. Woodhouse, *British Foreign Policy Since the Second World War* (London: Hutchinson, 1961) pp.87–8
54. Robert Hewison, *In Anger: Culture in the Cold War 1945–60* (London: Weidenfeld and Nicolson, 1981) pp.23–4
55. Robert Taylor, 'The Campaign for Nuclear Disarmament' in Bogdanor and Skidelsky, op. cit., p.223
56. J.B. Priestley, 'Britain and the Nuclear Bombs', *New Statesman*, 2 November 1957, pp.554–6
57. Quoted in Taylor, op. cit., p.225
58. Mervyn Jones, *Chances: An Autobiography* (London: Verso, 1987) p.148
59. Lewis, op. cit., p.100
60. Jeff Nutall, *Bomb Culture* (London:

MacGibbon and Kee, 1968) p.45

61. Michael Foot, *Tribune*, 11 October 1957

62. Priestley, op. cit., p.556

63. Nutall, op. cit., p.46

64. Quoted in Robert Hewison, op. cit., pp. 201–2

65. Quoted in Brian Masters, *The Swinging Sixties* (London: Constable, 1985) pp.202–3

66. *New Statesman*, 21 June 1958, p.799

67. Taylor, op. cit., p.222

68. Nutall, op. cit., p.47

69. In 1961 a crowd of 12,000 gathered in Trafalgar Square and thousands staged a sit-down protest; 1,314 people were arrested and there was considerable police brutality – a foretaste of the anti-Vietnam demonstrations at the end of the decade.

AFFLUENCE

1. 'Boom', *Queen*, 15 September 1959

2. Quoted in Peter Lewis, *The Fifties* (London: Heinemann, 1978) p.38

3. Anthony Sampson, *Anatomy of Britain* (London: Hodder and Stoughton, 1962) p.636

4. Peter Clarke, *Hope and Glory. Britain 1900–1990* (Harmondsworth: Penguin, 1996) p.255

5. Anthony Sampson, *Macmillan: A Study in Ambiguity* (London: Allen Lane, 1967) p.158

6. Ibid., p. 241

7. Jocelyn Stevens, 'Mac the Man', *Queen*, May 1963

8. 'Standardisation and Socialism', in MacDonald and Porter, *Putting on the Style*, unnumbered

9. Quoted in Lewis, op. cit., p.200

10. 'Room at the Top', MacDonald and Porter, op. cit.

11. Ibid.

12. *Woman*, 10 January 1959, pp.14–15

13. Clarke, op. cit., p.242

14. 'Traditional Values' in MacDonald and

Porter, op. cit.

15. Ibid.

16. London History Workshop, transcript of an interview with Terence Conran for *The Making of Modern London*, series 4, 16 April 1986, quoted in MacDonald and Porter, op. cit.

17. Geoffrey Gorer, *Exploring the English Character* (London: Cresset, 1955) p. 97

18. Quoted in Harry Hopkins, *The New Look: A Social History of the Forties and Fifties* (London: Secker and Warburg, 1964) p.320

19. Ibid, p.310

20. Lewis, op. cit., p.30

21. Hopkins, op. cit., p.331

22. Trevor Evans, *Ernest Bevin* (London: Allen and Unwin, 1946)

23. Hopkins, op. cit., p.328

24. Lewis, op. cit., p.31

25. Jane Dorner, *Fashion in the Forties and Fifties* (London: Ian Allen Ltd, 1975) p.52

26. Ibid.

27. Lewis, op. cit., p.219

28. Ibid., p.208

29. Ibid.

30. Hopkins, op. cit., p.403

31. Lewis op. cit., p.209

32. Ross McKibben, *Classes and Cultures: England 1918–1951* (Oxford: Oxford University Press, 1998) p.419

33. Len Deighton, *The Ipcress File* (London: Hodder and Stoughton, 1962)

34. Arthur Marwick, *British Society since 1945* (Harmondsworth: Penguin, third edition, 1996) pp.32–3

35. Ibid., p.117

36. Harry Hopkins, *The New Look: A Social History of the '40s and '50s* (London: Secker and Warburg, 1964) pp.461–2

37. Sampson, op. cit., p.159

38. Jocelyn Stevens, *Introduction to the Sixties in Queen* (eds.) Nicholas Coleridge and Stephen Quinn (London: Ebury Press, 1987) pp. 8–18

YOUTHQUAKE

1. Christopher Booker, *The Neophiliacs: A Study of the Revolution in English Life in the Fifties and Sixties* (London: Collins, 1959) p.138

2. 'Farewell to the Fifties', leader in the *Economist*, 26 December 1959, p.3

3. Viscount Kilmuir, *Political Adventures* (London: Weidenfeld and Nicolson, 1964) p.321

4. *Queen*, August 1959

5. Jocelyn Stevens, 'The Queen and I' in Nicholas Coleridge and Stephen Quinn (eds), *The Sixties in Queen* (London: Ebury Press, 1987) pp.9–10

6. 'The Establishment Chronicle', *Queen*, August 1959

7. 'A Bad Year for Dodos', *Queen*, December 1959

8. *Queen*, 17 April 1962

9. John Osborne, 'They Call It Cricket' in Tom Maschler (ed.), *Declaration* (London: McGibbon Kee, 1957) pp.80–1

10. Terence Rattigan's introduction to the 1953 edition of the second volume of his *Selected Plays*, quoted in Hewison, *In Anger*, pp.77–8

11. Jeff Nutall, *Bomb Culture*, p.55

12. Quoted in Booker, op. cit., p.110

13. *Observer*, 1954, quoted in Booker, op. cit., pp.91–2

14. Ibid., p.121

15. Colin Wilson, 'Beyond the Outsider' in Maschler, op. cit., p.35

16. Quoted in Peter Lewis, *The Fifties*, p.166

17. Quoted in Hewison, op. cit., p.151

18. John Wain, 'Along the Tightrope' in Maschler, op. cit., p.106

19. Quoted in Lewis, op. cit., p.162

20. Quoted in Hewison, op. cit., p.154

21. Brian Masters, *The Swinging Sixties* (London: Constable, 1985) pp.155–6

22. Patrick Marnham, *The Private Eye Story* (London: André Deutsch, 1982) p.24

23. Ibid.

24. Maschler, op. cit., p.76

25. Quoted in Lewis, op. cit., p.184

26. Masters, op. cit., p.187

27. 'Debs with a Difference', *Queen*, April 1962

28. John Crosby, 'London, the Most Exciting City in the World', *Weekend Telegraph*, 16 April 1965

29. Quoted in Masters, op. cit., p.157

30. *Private Eye*, March 1963

31. Booker, op. cit., p.209

32. *Queen*, March 1961

33. Labour Party Political Broadcast, 15 July 1964

34. 'London, The Most Exciting City in the World', *Weekend Telegraph*, 30 April 1965

35. *Quant by Quant* (London: Pan Books, 1965)

36. Ibid., p.40

37. Alexandra Pringle, 'Chelsea Girl' in Sara Maitland (ed.), *Very Heaven: Looking Back at the 1960s* (London: Virago, 1988) p.36

38. Felicity Green, 'Four girls prove that beauty and business ideas can go together', *Daily Mirror*, 4 May 1963

39. *New Statesman*, 29 May 1964

40. David Bailey and Peter Evans, *Goodbye Baby and Amen: A Saraband for the Sixties* (London: Condé Nast Publications in association with Wm Collins, 1969) p.5

41. Jacket blurb to David Bailey and Francis Wyndham, *A Box of Pin Ups* (London: Condé Nast in association with Wm Collins, 1965)

42. Barty Phillips, *Conran and the Habitat Story* (London: Weidenfeld and Nicolson, 1984) p.28

43. Lewis, op. cit., p.124

44. A. Bicat, 'Fifties Children: Sixties People' in ibid Bogdanor and Skidelsky, *The Age of Affluenc*e, p.324

45. George Melly, *Revolt into Style* (London: Allen Lane, 1970)

46. Lewis, op. cit., p.142

47. Colin MacInnes, *Absolute Beginners* (London: MacGibbon and Kee, 1959)

48. Nutall, op. cit., p.35

49. Philip Norman, *Shout! The Beatles in Their Generation* (London: Elm Tree Books, 1982) p.56

50. Quoted in Masters, op. cit., p.168; *The Times*, 10 December 1980

51. Samuel H. Beer, *Britain Against Itself: The Political Consequences of Collectivism* (London: Faber and Faber, 1982) p.139

52. Robert Hewison, *Too Much: Art and Society in the Sixties: 1960–1975* (London: Methuen, 1986) p.66

53. Brian Epstein, quoted in Bailey and Evans, op. cit., p.73

54. John Lennon in an interview with *Rolling Stone*, 1970, quoted in Ian MacDonald, *Revolution in the Head: The Beatles' Records and the Sixties* (London: Fourth Estate, 1994) p.2

55. Patrick O'Donovan, 'The Funeral of Winston Churchill', *Observer*, 31 January 1965

56. Ibid.

57. Philip Larkin, 'Annus Mirabilis' in *High Windows* (London: Faber and Faber, 1974)

58. John Osborne, *Inadmissible Evidence* (London: Faber and Faber, 1965)

BIBLIOGRAPHY

The numerous rich sources – histories, biographies, autobiographies, memoirs and reminiscences, novels and poems – for this book are too numerous to mention here, but are evidenced in the Notes. There are, however, a number of histories of the twentieth century – or part of that century – which form an essential starting point for its comprehension. They are listed below, in alphabetical order according to the author's surname.

Vernon Bogdanor and Robert Skidelsky (eds), *The Age of Affluence, 1951–1964* (Basingstoke: Macmillan, 1970)

Peter Calvocoressi, *The British Experience, 1945–75* (London: Bodley Head, 1978)

Peter Clarke, *Hope and Glory: Britain 1900–1990* (Harmondsworth: Penguin, 1996)

Peter Hennessy, *Never Again: Britain 1945–1951* (London: Jonathan Cape, 1992)

Ross McKibben, *Classes and Cultures: England 1918–1951* (Oxford: Oxford University Press, 1998)

Arthur Marwick, *British Society since 1945* (Harmondsworth: Penguin, third edition, 1996)

Arthur Marwick, *The Sixties* (Oxford: Oxford University Press, 1998)

Kenneth O. Morgan, *The People's Peace: British History, 1945–1989* (Oxford: Oxford University Press, 1990)

Michael Sissons and Philip French (eds), *The Age of Austerity: 1945–1951* (London: Hodder and Stoughton, 1963)

index

acknowledgements

This book is for Sarah, who helped particularly.

I would like to thank the family, friends and colleagues with whom I have discussed this enterprise exhaustively and who have read parts of it, and held views on all. At Collins & Brown I would like to thank Mark Collins, Colin Ziegler, Sarah Hoggett, Ginny Surtees, Alison Lee, Simon Brockbank, Claire Waite and Sonia Pugh for their help, Mandy Greenfield for copy editing and Philippa Lewis for picture research – and discussion. At the Imperial War Museum I am most grateful for the help of Christopher Dowling, Angela Godwin and Jan Mihell, and at Conran Design to James Soane.

PICTURE CREDITS
Illustrations on these pages appear by kind permission of the following:

Hardy Amis 44, 45; Akeburst Bureau © Lewis Morley 114 (top), 122, 129; BBC Archive 81 (bottom left and top right), 102 (both), 103, 104 (right), 124; The British Council, by kind permission of Patricia Bratby 15; CD Partnership 47 (bottom right); Corbis 10 (right), 14, 17 (bottom), 18, 32, 46 (bottom left), 47 (bottom right), 64 (bottom), 71, 78, 81 (centre), 95 (bottom), 99 (top), 107, 114/115 (background), 115 (bottom), 120, 135, 144 (right), 146, 151; Philippe Garner 80/81 (background), 80 (top and bottom left and top right), 84 (top), 89 (bottom), 90, 116, 132, 133, 134, 137, 145; Hulton Getty 2, 6, 9 (left), 10, 11 (background), 11, 12/13 (background), 12 (centre), 17 (top), 18, 20, 22 (bottom), 25, 30, 41 (bottom), 54, 55, 60 (top), 63, 64 (top), 66, 70, 76, 77, 80, 82, 86/87 (background) 87, 94 (right), 99 (bottom), 100, 101, 106 (left), 108, 109 (right), 112 (left), 127, 130, 141 (both), 146, 147 (background), 147, 149 (top), 150; Imperial War Museum 12 (right), 21, 22 (top), 73 (both); Philippa Lewis 3, 7, 12 (top left), 26 (bottom), 43, 46/47 (background), 46 (top left and centre), 48 (both), 50, 52/53 (background), 52, 57, 61 (both), 62 (both), 80 (centre), 81 (bottom right), 83, 84 (bottom), 88 (both), 89 (top), 93 (top left and right), 95 (top), 96, 98, 99 (background), 105, 109 (left), 114 (right), 117, 136, 138, 140; London Metropolitan Archive 53, 56, 58 (both), 59; Mander and Mitchenson Theatre Collection 81 (top left), 104 (left); National Magazine Company 112 (right), 113; Robert Opie 9 (right), 13 (bottom left and centre), 27, 28, 29, 33, 35 (left), 36, 38 (bottom), 40 (background), 46 (top right), 47 (top right), 60 (bottom), 65 (both), 68, 75 (top), 80 (bottom right), 81 (centre right), 91, 93 (bottom), 110, 114 (centre right), 115 (centre left), 144 (left), 148, 149 (bottom), 152; Private Collection, photo Hazlitt, Gooden & Fox, by kind permission of the artist's estate 15; Private Eye 118 (both), 123, 125; Ronald Grant Archive 10 (bottom left), 40, 42 (both), 69, 78 (top), 86, 94 (left), 106 (right), 121 (all), 139 (bottom); Stevenage Museum 26 (top); The Tate Gallery 142; Topham Picturepoint 5(all), 13 (right), 16, 23, 24, 31 (both), 34, 35 (right), 37, 38 (top), 39 (both), 41 (top), 49, 67, 74, 97, 98 (both), 139 (top); Whitford Fine Art Gallery, by kind permission of the artist's estate 115 (top right), 153; Val Wilmer 10 (top left), 75 (bottom).

These illustrations come from the following books:
p. 12 (bottom left) *Home Rails Preferred* by Emmett (Faber & Faber, 1948); p. 85 *London – So Help Me!* by Winifred Ellis, illustrations by Ronald Searle (Macdonald, 1952).